AMERICAN
WOODWORKER™

FURNITURE PROJECTS

```
3
MO    JY  2 '91
CO    AC 07 '90
KI    JE 13 '91
RI    NO 08 '91
SW    FE 06 '92
UP    OC 22 '92
- - - - - - - - - - - - - - - - - -
4
ER    JE  4 '89
CS    FE 22 '91
HL    OC 16 '90
PI    JE 01 '92
BE
BL    DE 21 '90
   SK    AG 06 '92
```

AMERICAN
WOODWORKER™

FURNITURE
PROJECTS

Rodale Press, Emmaus, Pennsylvania

Printed in the United States of America on acid- free paper
containing a high percentage of recycled fiber.

Library of Congress Cataloging-in-Publication Data
American woodworker furniture projects.
          p.   cm.
    On t.p. the registered trademark symbol "TM" is superscript
following "woodworker" in the title.
    ISBN 0-87857-793-9 paperback
    1. Furniture making – Amateurs' manuals.   I. American
woodworker.   II. Title: Furniture projects.
TT195.A47   1989
684.1'042 – dc19   88-28334
                                                                           CIP

2   4   6   8   10   9   7   5   3   1   paperback

Contents

Tea Cart
By Frank M. Pittman

Early American tea carts can be both useful and attractive additions to a home. They are actually small drop leaf tables on wheels, and it is important when designing one to design around the wheels. This means that you should have both the large wooden wheels and the casters on hand before beginning. I opted not to make the wooden wheels and purchased two cherry wheels (#90WP14) from Constantine, 2050 Eastchester Road, Bronx, N.Y. 10461. If you want to make your own wheels, you can find some helpful information in the old book, *The Art of Woodturning* by William W. Klenke. If you make your own wheels or purchase them from some other vendor, be sure to verify sizes on the drawing before beginning; you may need to alter some dimensions.

A few years ago I acquired some fifty year old air dried cherry, and I used some of it for this project. This wood was a joy to work with and has a beautiful natural color. Walnut or maple would also make an attractive cart.

CONSTRUCTION

Begin by turning the four legs. The turnings are relatively simple, requiring only a few caliper settings. Rails (parts E & F) can be made and joined to the legs. A hand cut dovetail joint is used on the top rail. I used a dovetail angle of 1″ in 6″ throughout this project.

Aprons (parts G & H) can be prepared and mortised into the legs. The lower rails (parts U & V) are mortised into the lower part of each leg. After all aprons and rails have been fitted the parts can be sanded and assembled with glue.

The outer side aprons and the hinged leaf supports are next. The simple wooden hinge I used isn't a very

"It is best to wait until the tops and leaves have been installed before making this knob..."

sophisticated model, but it works well and looks good. The knuckles were sawed out using a table saw to make the straight end cuts and a jig saw to saw out the bottom of each square cutout. After the knuckles are squared out, parts J and K can be clamped together and the ¼″ hole for the pivot rod can be drilled through both parts at the same time using a drill press. The knuckles on part J are rounded over on both surfaces, while part K knuckles only require rounding on the outer surface. Install a temporary ¼″ pin in the hinge and dry clamp parts I, J and K to the inner aprons (parts H) to check out everything, especially the swing of the leaf support. After these parts are fitted properly, they should be

(CONTINUED ON PAGE 12)

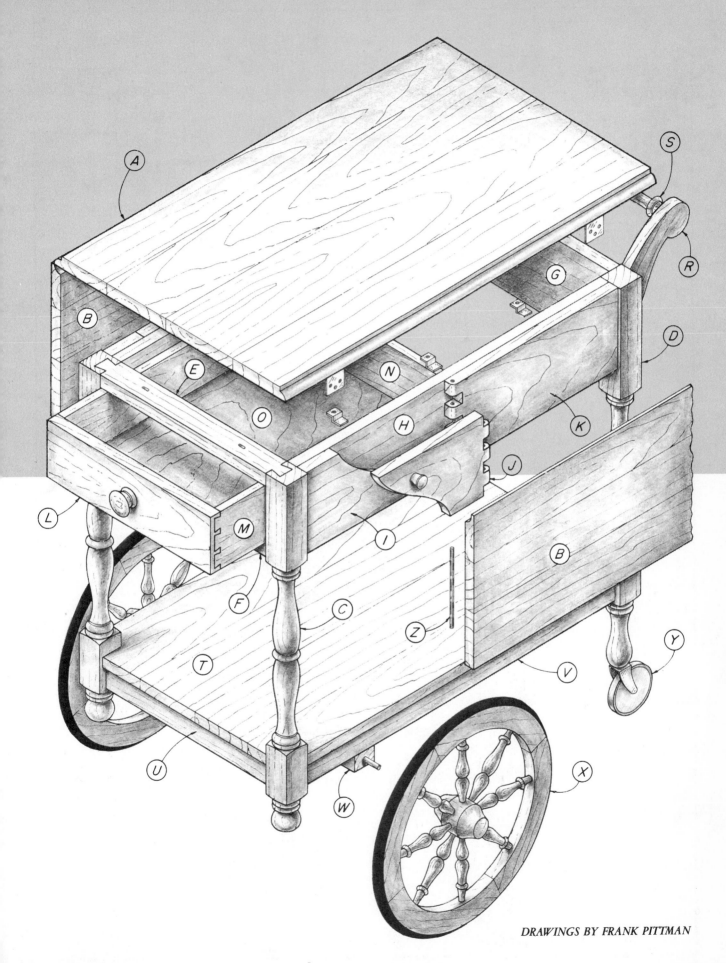

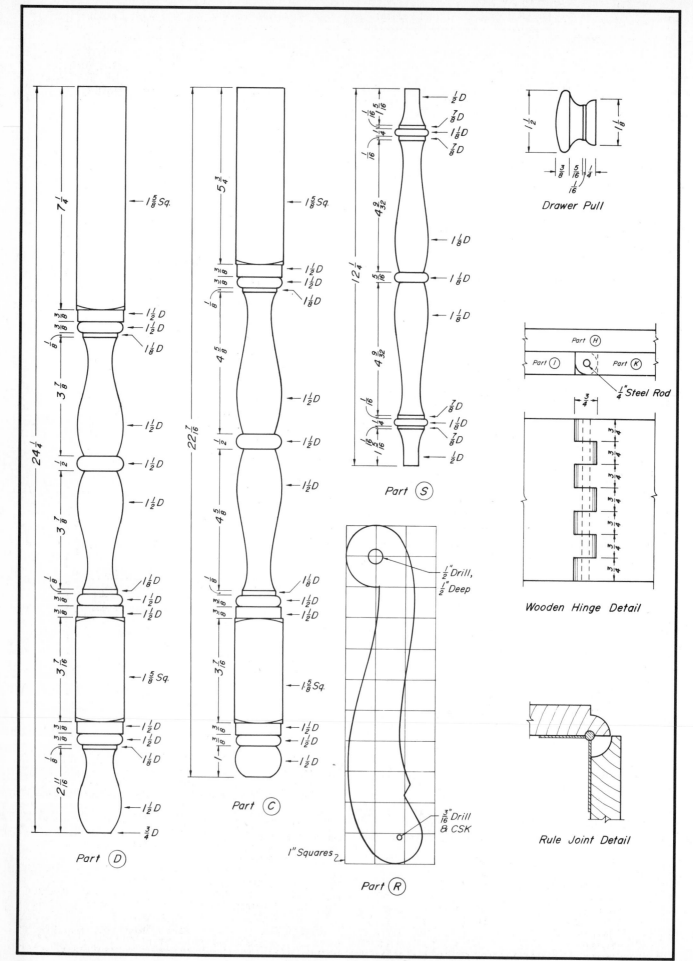

Part D

Part C

Part S

Part R

Drawer Pull

Wooden Hinge Detail

Rule Joint Detail

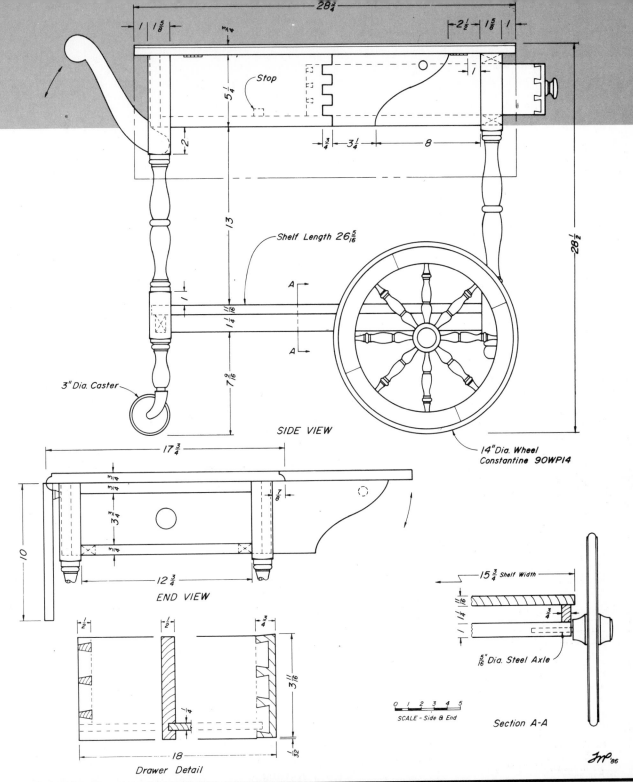

SIDE VIEW

Shelf Length 26 5/16

3" Dia. Caster

14" Dia. Wheel
Constantine 90WP14

END VIEW

15 3/4 Shelf Width

5/16" Dia. Steel Axle

Section A-A

0 1 2 3 4 5
SCALE - Side & End

Drawer Detail

JMP '86

Bill Of Material

CODE	DESCRIPTION	QTY.	T	W	L	CODE	DESCRIPTION	QTY.	T	W	L
A	Top	1	3/4"	17 3/4"	28 3/4"	N	Drawer back	1	1/2"	3 3/16"	12 11/16"
B	Leaf	2	3/4"	10"	28 3/4"	O	Drawer bottom	1	1/4"	12 3/16"	17 1/2"
C	Leg (short)	2	1 5/8"	1 5/8"	22 7/16"	P	Drawer slide	2	3/4"	1"	24"
D	Leg (long)	2	1 5/8"	1 5/8"	24 1/4"	Q	Drawer stop	2	3/4"	1"	1"
E	Rail	1	3/4"	1 5/8"	14 1/4"	R	Handle support	2	3/4"	3"	11"
F	Rail	1	3/4"	1 5/8"	14 1/4"	S	Handle turning	1	1 1/4"	1 1/4"	13"
G	End apron	1	3/4"	5 1/4"	14"	T	Shelf	1	11/16"	15 3/4"	26 5/16"
H	Side apron (inner)	2	3/4"	5 1/4"	24 3/4"	U	End shelf support	2	3/4"	1 1/4"	14"
I	Short side apron	2	3/4"	5 1/4"	8"	V	Side shelf support	2	3/4"	1 1/4"	24 3/4"
J	Leaf support	2	3/4"	5 1/4"	9 1/2"	W	Axle support	1	1"	1 1/2"	15 1/4"
K	Long side apron	2	3/4"	5 1/4"	12 1/4"	X	Wheels	2	14" diameter		
L	Drawer front	1	3/4"	3 11/16"	12 11/16"	Y	Casters	2	3" diameter		
M	Drawer side	2	1/2"	3 11/16"	17 3/4"	Z	Hinge pivot	2	1/4" x 5 1/4" steel		

sanded through 220 grit. Butt glue parts I and K to the inner aprons. The small knob which is screwed to the leaf support also serves as a leaf stop, keeping the leaves in a vertical position when they are down. It is best to wait until the top and leaves have been installed before making this knob since the distance from the inner part of the leaf to the top surface of the knob is critical.

DRAWER

The drawer is a rather straight forward flush drawer with dovetailed front and back. The drawer bottom, which was made from ¼" birch plywood, was grooved in all the way around. It is important in flush drawer construction to create a uniform gap around the front. A gap of 1/32" to 1/16" all the way around is sufficient for a drawer as small as this one. I did not use a "kicker" rail above the drawer (a rail to prevent the drawer from tipping downward as it is opened). The drawer does tip down slightly but not severely. You could easily add a kicker by screwing a strip to the underside of the top.

The 1" wide drawer slides were butt glued to the inner aprons, and drawer stop blocks were located and glued to the slides. The drawer pull was turned using a screw center and was mounted with one #10 x 1½" FH brass screw.

WHEELS & CASTERS

The wheels I purchased were only partially sanded, and it took quite a while to hand sand them to an acceptable stage. They also contained some unwanted sapwood, so I stained the sapwood and the entire wheel to make it match the old cherry I was using. The rubber tires should be removed while sanding and finishing.

The axles were made from two 5/16" diameter cold rolled steel rods approximately 5" long. I would be tempted to buy them with the wheels next time (Constantine sells axles, also). The ends of the axle blanks had to be shaped to prevent the wheels from coming off too easily. You can determine the length of axle projection by fitting each rod to the wheels before mounting them to the axle support board (part W). A 5/16" hole can be drilled in each end of part W to the depth which would yield the proper projection. The axle blanks were glued into the support piece with an epoxy adhesive.

Casters are installed by drilling holes for the caster anchors in the end of the turnings and carefully tapping the anchors in place with a hammer. The size of the anchor hole is critical, because you certainly don't want to split the end of the turning.

Install the casters temporarily and place the wheel / axle assembly in place under rails (parts V). With the wheels and casters in place, measure the height of the cart from the floor on both ends and from side to side. Slight variations of 1/16" or less are probably acceptable. You can add shims or remove wood from the axle support piece to level the cart. After leveling, part W can be screwed and glued to the underside of the rails using four #8 x 1½" FH screws.

TOP, LEAVES & SHELF

The top, leaves and shelf were made using edge butt joints on stock no wider than 4". The rule joint was cut on a shaper using a special rule joint knife. Four special drop leaf table hinges were used. I did not gain-in the hinges as some do. I don't like to see the gain on the rule joint when the leaf

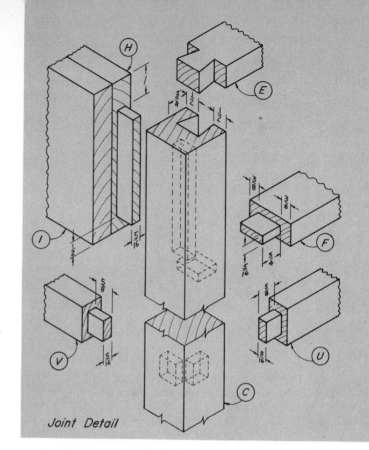

Joint Detail

is down. I simply cut a recess for the hinge knuckle into the top so it will be flush with the underside of the top and leaf. When locating the hinges, it is important that the center of the pin be located in line with the shoulder of the joint (see the rule joint detail). The top is attached with metal table top clips and two #8 x 1¼" FH screws through the slotted holes in rail E.

The shelf should be squared to finished size, 15¾" x 26 5/16". Carefully layout the cutouts for each leg and cut them by hand or use a band saw. The shelf should have approximately 3/32" clearance at each leg to allow for expansion. Sand the shelf through 220 grit and install it with metal table top clips.

HANDLE

The handle or towel rack which is made from parts R and S is next. I made the handle so it would pivot. It is fastened to the legs with two #10 x 1½" FH brass screws. Notice in the drawing and the photograph that the handle side supports are made with a small shoulder which catches the bottom of the apron when the cart is pushed. Most of the time the handle is hanging down between the legs.

FINISHING

Removing the leaf support, handle, drawer, leaves, wheels and top before finishing makes things easier. The cart was finished with lacquer with the final coat being rubbed with 0000 steel wool to produce a satin sheen.

About the Author

Frank M. Pittman is an associate editor for **The American Woodworker.**

Small Cherry Drop-Leaf Table

by Franklin H. Gottshall

The small drop-leaf table, shown in Fig. 1, is well proportioned, and of a convenient size to be used as a kitchen table or in a small dining area. Cherry is the wood recommended to build the table, and is indeed the wood used for the top, drop-leaves, and drawer front of the table shown in the photographs. However, as was often the case on small country-made tables in this category, the legs, sides and other parts of this table were made of poplar, and colored with a cherry oil stain to resemble the more desirable material used for the top and leaves.

To build the table, cut and square up stock for the four legs. Dimensions to turn these and cut mortises are shown in Fig. 3. The right front leg is like the left front except that mortises which are shown on the right of the square part in Fig. 3, will be moved to replace those on the left side, while those on the left side in Fig. 3 will be moved to the right side. All mortises on both back legs will be like those on the right side of the square section in Fig. 3. Mortises on all four legs are 5/16'' wide and 1-3/8'' deep, and should be laid out and cut before turning the legs on the lathe. Side rails (B), back rail (C), and rails (D) and (E) should be made, and tenons fitted to mortises before turning the legs.

Figures 4, 5, and 6, show the assembled table. Figures 4 and 5 show the table with one leaf dropped, and the raised leaf held in a horizontal position by support strip (F), which can be rotated as shown on the right in Fig. 4 to support the leaf. By swinging the support strip back, parallel with the side rail where it is held in place with a 20-penny nail acting as a fulcrum, the leaf may be dropped to hang vertically, as shown on the left of Figures 4 and 5. When both leaves are dropped into this position, the table occupies only one-third as much space in a room as it does with both leaves extended. This is a desirable feature where space is limited. The small drawer has sufficient storage area to hold flat tableware and napkins.

FIG. 1

Drop-leaves are joined to the table top with rule joints, these being closed joints at all times, making them a much more desirable joint for this purpose than ordinary butt joints. A special type of hinge is used for this kind of joint, like the ones shown in Fig. 7. Matched shaper cutters, having a one-half inch radius, are usually used to cut the bead and matching groove for this joint. On a top 7/8'' thick, like the top of this table, this leaves the upper 3/8'' edge of the joint on the leaf thick and sturdy. If thinner boards are used to make such a top, the cutter radius should be reduced in size.

It should be noted that the hinge is set into the leaf and table top to make it flush with undersides of both, and that the barrel of the hinge joint must be centered exactly below the point shown in Fig. 7 to properly align the joint.

Fig. 8 shows construction of the table frame in greater detail than it can be shown in Figures 4, 5, and 6. It shows both leaf support strips in the position they would be in with the leaves dropped. Blocks (P) and (Q) are shown here with both ends of the leaf support strips butted against them. These are fastened to the table sides (B) with glue and wood screws, and have holes drilled through them for wood screws used to hold the table top and frame together. Strips (R) at both ends of the table frame serve the same purpose.

Fig. 9 shows dimensions and details to make the small drawer. The front and

FIG. 2

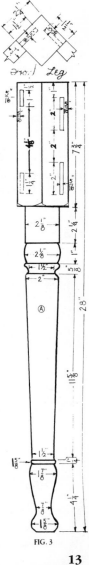

FIG. 3

back of the drawer are dovetailed to the drawer sides. Hand-made dovetails on old work are made with tails on drawer sides much wider than the pins found on the front and back. The drawer front (G) is curved so that it protrudes ½'' beyond the frame when the drawer is pushed back into the table as far as it will go, as shown in Fig. 10. Dimensions for laying out the dovetail joints are shown in the enlarged drawings at the upper right in Fig. 9. The turned wooden knob is fastened to the drawer front with glue and a wood screw. While drawer bottoms on old pieces of furniture like this table were made of solid wood, the plywood recommended here is better, because it does not swell or shrink because of atmospheric changes of seasons, and therefore, exerts no pressure on drawer sides to loosen drawer joints. The thinner bottom also reduces weight and increases storage capacity inside the drawer.

After all parts of the table have been assembled and all surfaces have been sanded smooth, the table is ready for applying coats of finish. Cherry colored oil stain is recommended. It should be brushed on and wiped dry as possible with clean cotton cloths immediately after a surface has been covered. On cherry wood, one application should be enough to color the wood but, if a lighter colored wood like poplar is used, a second application of stain may be necessary after the first coat has dried in order to achieve the desired hue. Allow oil stain to dry at least 48 hours in a warm, dry room. When the stain has thoroughly dried, mix equal parts of a good grade of glossy floor varnish with spirits of turpentine and apply it over the stained surface as a sealer to hold the stain. To prevent lifting stain, do not brush the surface excessively. The sealer coat should be followed with at least two more coats of full-bodied varnish.

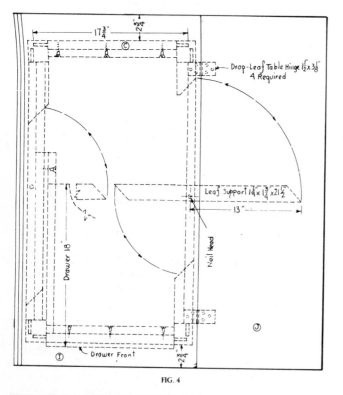

FIG. 4

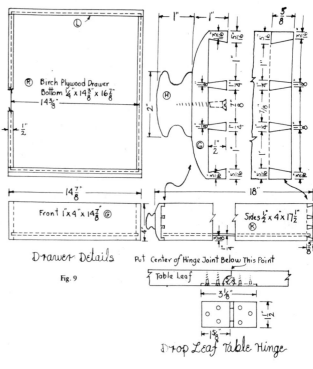

Drawer Details

Fig. 9

Drop Leaf Table Hinge

FIG. 7

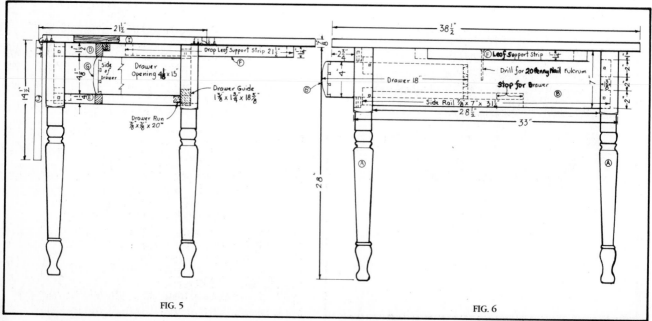

FIG. 5

FIG. 6

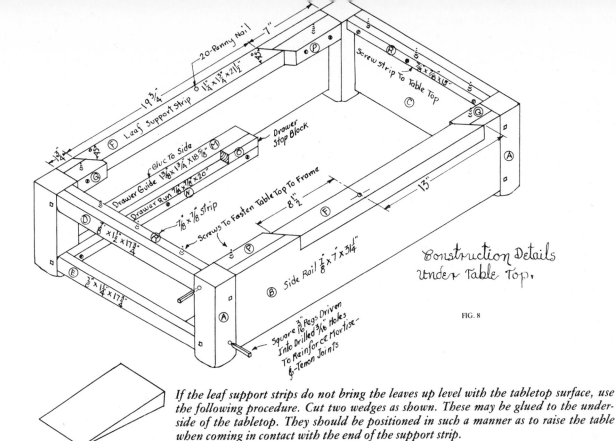

Construction Details
under Table Top.

FIG. 8

If the leaf support strips do not bring the leaves up level with the tabletop surface, use the following procedure. Cut two wedges as shown. These may be glued to the underside of the tabletop. They should be positioned in such a manner as to raise the table when coming in contact with the end of the support strip.

After each coat of varnish has dried thoroughly, it should be smoothed down with .00 steel wool and open-coat garnet paper, #2/0 or finer grit. Varnish should be applied to both inside and outside surfaces of the table. After smoothing down each coat, remove all dust carefully. If necessary, use a damp cloth after first dusting with a brush, and when dry, apply the succeeding coat.

If the final coat is to be rubbed smooth with powdered pumice stone and rubbing oil, three coats of glossy varnish should be applied first. The pumice and oil rub may then be done on flat surfaces with a small piece of rubbing felt measuring about 3'' x 5''. Turned, carved surfaces and moldings will have to be rubbed with soft, clean cotton cloths.

A good durable substitute for a hand-rubbed final coat may be had by using satin finish varnish for the final coat. This dries to a duller semi-gloss as it dries, and nothing more need be done to it once a coat has been applied.

Fig. 10

Small Cherry Drop-Leaf Table

CHERRY
(A) 4 legs 2¼" x 2¼" x 28"
(B) 2 side rails 7/8" x 7" x 31¼"
(C) 1 back rail 7/8" x 7" x 17¾"
(D) 1 rail above drawer 7/8" x 1½" x 17¾"
(E) 1 rail below drawer 7/8" x 1¼" x 17¾"
(F) 2 leaf support strips 1¼" x 1¾" x 21½"
(G) 1 drawer front 1" x 4" x 14 7/8"
(H) 1 drawer pull 1" x 2" diam.
(I) 1 table top 7/8" x 21½" x 38½"
(J) 2 table leaves 7/8" x 14½" x 38½"

POPLAR
(K) 2 drawer sides ½" x 4" x 17½"
(L) 1 drawer back 5/8" x 4" x 14 7/8"
(M) 2 drawer guides 1 3/8" x 1¾" x 18 5/8"
(N) 2 drawer runs 7/8" x 7/8" x 20"
(O) 2 drawer stops 7/8" x 7/8" x 3¼"
(P) 2 blocks under top 1¼" x 1 3/8" x 6¼"
(Q) 2 blocks under top 1¼" x 1 3/8" x 3¼"
(R) 2 strips to fasten top to table frame
     7/8" x 7/8" x 15"

BIRCH PLYWOOD
(S) 1 drawer bottom ¼" x 14 3/8" x 16 7/8"

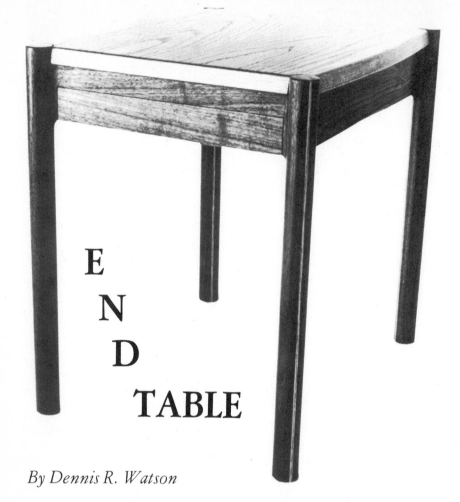

Walnut and white oak combined with clean simple lines produce an attractive contemporary end table. The small drawer, which is almost hidden, makes the table very practical sitting by a couch or easy chair.

E
N
D
TABLE

By Dennis R. Watson

The legs are the first order of business; begin by selecting 8/4 (1¾ inch thick) walnut. Rip the leg 1¾ inches square and crosscut to 22 inches in length; the extra length will be trimmed off after turning. The next step is to rip the leg on the diagonal. This is easily done on the bandsaw with a "V" guide board (Fig. 1). Remove the saw marks by either hand planing or running the edges over the jointer, removing as little wood as possible.

Rip a piece of white oak 1/8 inch thick by 2¾ inches wide (Fig. 2), then hand plane or joint to remove the saw marks. Apply glue and clamp the white oak strip between the walnut sides; there is a tendency for the boards to slip when clamping pressure is applied so try to keep the leg square in cross section. After the glue has dried trim the oak strip flush with the walnut sides.

FIG. 1. *To rip the leg across the diagonal, clamp a "V" block to the bandsaw table. Set the guides low and use a sharp blade.*

FIG. 2.
The 1/8 inch thick strip of white oak for the legs is easily resawn on the bandsaw using a simple round nose guide. Cut the strip a little over 1/8 inch thick, then plane the saw marks off.

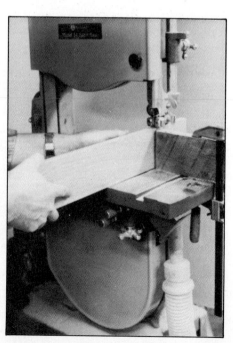

Mark the center of the leg accurately and install between centers in the lathe. When turning the leg, turn about 1½ inches in length on the top. Leave a square section about four inches long, then turn the remaining bottom portion.

After turning all four legs, lay out the location of the mortises and mark the exact length of the leg. I cut the mortises on a radial arm saw with a ¼ inch bottoming end mill in the right hand chuck. Cut the

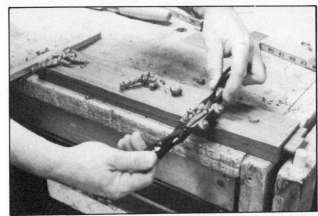

FIG. 3. *Shape the lower edge of the side aprons with a spokeshave. The chamfer is about ¼ inch wide at the middle tapering off to nothing at the ends.*

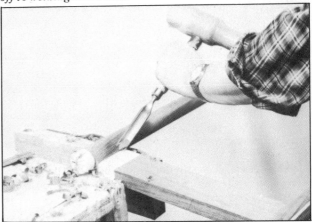

FIG. 4. *A carving gouge is used to rough shape the leg where it joins the apron. The remaining portion of the leg is lathe turned.*

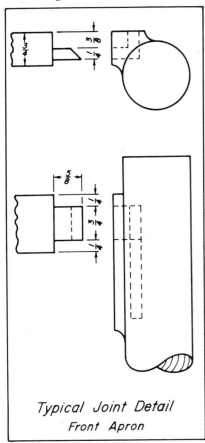

Typical Joint Detail
Front Apron

legs to length, being careful because the wood has a tendency to splinter. You can knife around the leg or wrap it with masking tape to reduce the splintering.

Cut the aprons to length; be sure to allow for the length of the tenons. The tenons are easily cut on the table saw using the sliding tenoning jig described in the June 1985 issue of *The American Woodworker.* Cut the tenon in a scrap piece and try the fit; it should be snug but not so tight that you have to drive it home.

Lay out the location of the drawer runner on the side rail and run a ½ x ¼ inch groove. Chamfer the bottom edge of the side apron with a spokeshave (Fig. 3). Now dry fit the base together. When all the joints pull up tightly, apply glue and allow to dry overnight, making sure the base is square.

The next step is to shape the square portion of the leg. Remove the bulk of the wood with a carving gouge (Fig. 4). A round surform is handy for smoothing the gouge marks out and final shaping (Fig. 5). Finish up with sandpaper. When shaping the leg use some masking tape to protect the turned part of the leg and apron.

FIG. 5. *A surform is used to smooth the carving marks left by the gouge. Masking tape protects the leg and apron.*

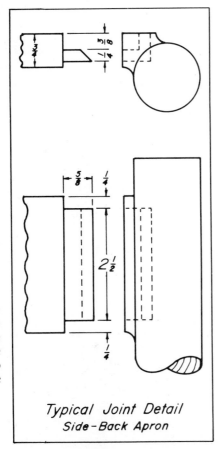

Typical Joint Detail
Side-Back Apron

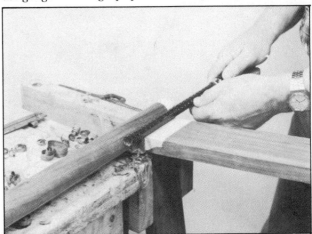

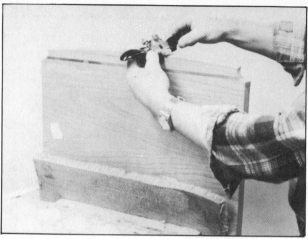

FIG. 6. Bandsaw the sides of the top, staying just to the outside of the line. Use a spokeshave to taper the sides and remove the saw marks.

The drawer is the next order of business. Construction is typical with blind dovetails used for the front and through dovetails for the rear. The dovetails can be hand cut, (see the March 1985 issue of *The American Woodworker*) or machine cut. Rip the sides and back from ½ inch oak, maple, or poplar, and crosscut to length. The drawer front should be cut from the same board as the front apron so the grain matches. Run a ¼ x ¼ inch groove in the front and sides for the ¼ inch plywood bottom, and a ½ x ¼ inch groove in the side for the runner. Glue and clamp the drawer together using the bottom to keep it square. After the glue has dried, screw the bottom to the back with several small flat head screws.

Install the drawer runner in the side apron using No. 4 x 1 inch flat head screws. Try the drawer; you can adjust the runner out by adding paper or cardboard shims, or if necessary, plane a little off the runner if the drawer is too tight. Add some paraffin to make the drawer slide smoothly. Push the drawer in all the way, then plane or sand the front so it lines up with the apron.

The top is made from ¾ inch plywood veneered with white oak and edged with hardwood. If you choose to use solid wood for the top be sure and make the gap betwen the leg and top large enough to allow the top to move with humidity changes. The plywood should be similar to birch or mahogany. Stay away from fir because the wild grain pattern will telegraph through the white oak veneer. Before ap-

FIG. 7. Remove the wood for the legs, staying outside of the marking. Finish up with a drum sander; try the fit frequently. Carpet is used to protect the top from vise marks.

plying the veneer, glue a ¼ x¾ inch solid white oak strip to the front and rear edges and plane or sand flush with the plywood. Apply the veneer and trim flush with the plywood. Using a fine tooth blade, rip a little off each side of the top to arrive at the final size.

Rip two strips of walnut ¼ inch wide and two strips of white oak two inches wide, and glue to each edge of the top. Very carefully plane or sand flush with the veneer.

The sides of the top are curved slightly which is easily cut on the bandsaw or with a saber saw. Smooth up the edges with a spokeshave (Fig. 6). Set the top in place and very accurately mark the location of each leg. Using a bandsaw or saber saw cut just at the outside of the lines. Try the top and make small adjustments to the cut-out using a small drum sander, about 1¼ inch diameter (Fig. 7). Try the fit frequently. Attach the ¾ x ¾ inch square ledger strip to the apron with No. 6 x 1¼ flat head screws, then screw the top to the ledger strip using the same size screws.

Give the table a thorough sanding with 220 grit paper (Fig. 8). Two coats of natural Watco Danish Oil were applied. The second coat was wet sanded with No. 600 wet dry paper. A coat of paste wax finishes the project.

FIG. 8. A sharp cabinet scraper is used to finish the white oak veneer top. This is a much safer method than using a belt sander on 1/28 inch thick veneer.

CUTTING LIST

Key	Qty.	Size	Description
A	4	1¾" x 1¾" x 20½"	Walnut leg
B	2	¾" x 3" x 19½"	Walnut side apron
C	1	¾" x 1¼" x 14½"	Walnut front apron
D	1	¾" x 3" x 14½"	Walnut rear apron
E	1	¾" x 14" x 20"	Plywood top
F	2	¼" x ¾" x 20½"	Walnut strip
G	2	¾" x 1 1/8" x 20½"	White oak edging
H	4	1/8" x 2¾" x 20½"	White oak strip
I	2	¾" x ¾" x 11¾"	Oak ledger
J	2	¾" x ¾" x 18¼"	Oak ledger
K	2	½" x 1¾" x 17"	Oak drawer sides
L	1	½" x 1¼" x 13 1/8"	Oak drawer back
M	1	¾" x 1¾" x 13 1/8"	Walnut drawer front
N	1	¼" x 12 5/8" x 17"	Plywood drawer bottom
O	2	½" x ½" x 16½"	Drawer runner
P	2	¼" x ¾" x 14"	White oak strip top

*Dennis R. Watson is a contributing editor to **The American Woodworker**.*

WALNUT-OAK TABLE

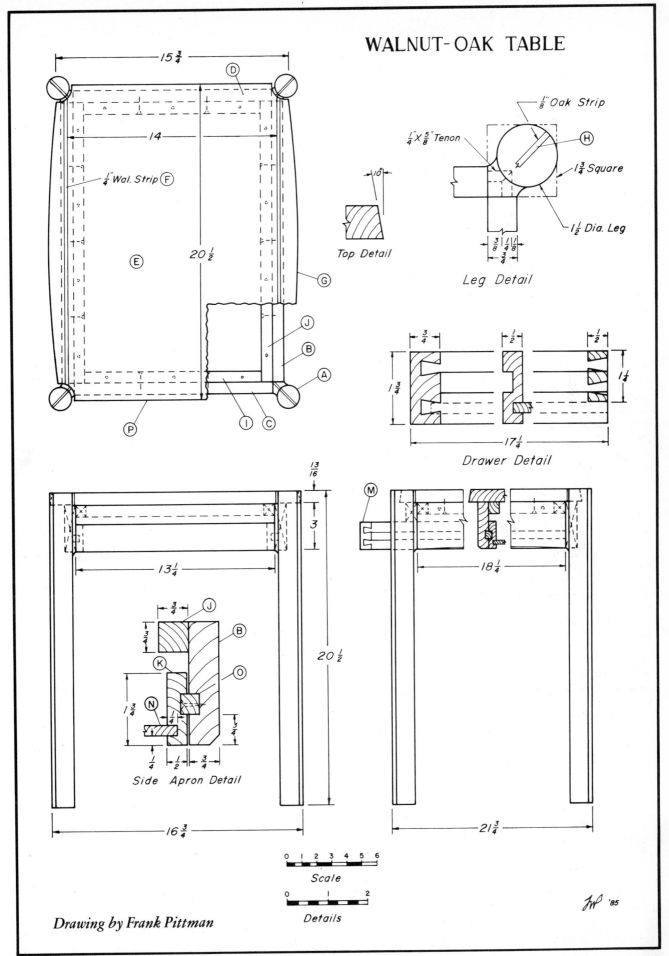

15¾

14

¼" Wal. Strip Ⓕ

20½

Ⓓ

Ⓔ

Ⓖ

Ⓙ

Ⓑ

Ⓐ

Ⓟ

Ⓘ Ⓒ

Top Detail

10°

⅛" Oak Strip

¼" X ⅝" Tenon

Ⓗ

1¾ Square

1½ Dia. Leg

⅜ 1¼⅛
¾

Leg Detail

¾ ½ ½

1¾ 1¼

17¼

Drawer Detail

13/16

3

13¼

20½

16¾

¾

Ⓙ

Ⓑ

¾
¾

Ⓚ

Ⓝ

Ⓞ

1¾

¼

¼ ½ ¾ ¾

Side Apron Detail

Ⓜ

18¼

21¾

0 1 2 3 4 5 6

Scale

0 1 2

Details

Drawing by Frank Pittman

ℐⱳℙ '85

Hepplewhite End Table

By Frank M. Pittman

The clean lines and delicate inlay of the Hepplewhite style adapt well to end or small bed-side tables. We have used a table similar to the one described in this article as a project for beginning woodworking students at Western Kentucky University for the past 20 years. The design has been modified slightly several times over the years.

Mahogany should be your first choice for a primary wood for this table. The secondary woods could be poplar, oak, or some other convenient hardwood. I actually used cherry for the drawer sides and back in the table pictured.

Construction should begin with the legs. 8/4 mahogany will comfortably produce the 1 - 5/8'' x 1 - 5/8'' squares. After the leg stock is squared to finished length (27 ¼'') carefully lay off the tapers. First locate a center line on two opposite faces of each leg. Lay off the 5/8'' leg width at the lower end. Measure down 5½'' from the top of each leg and square a line around the entire leg at this point. Connect 5/8'' points to 5½'' points with a straight line. Layout only on two opposite sides of each leg now. If you did the entire layout now part of it would be lost in the tapering operation.

Next cut the two opposing tapers on each leg. Several techniques could be used to produce the tapers. I will usually bandsaw the excess wood away and then either use a hand plane or a jointer to true them up. It is important, regardless of the method used, that the tapered surfaces be square and straight and that the taper not extend above the 5½'' line.

Next layout tapers on the new surfaces formed on each leg and cut these tapers as before. At this point you should have four legs which are tapered on all four sides. Choose the best looking pair of legs from the four and use them in front.

Inlaying the front legs is next. Only the fronts of the front legs were inlaid on this table. However, you could inlay the front and sides of all legs if you like. Some Hepplewhite furniture is ornamented this way and I have done it before on this table.

Years ago we used a scratching tool (a modified marking gauge) to cut the slots for inlay. Today, however, I recommend cutting the slots with a router and a 1/16'' straight bit. I usually use a router table with a fence and an inverted portable router to make these cuts. I set up the router fence so as to position the bit 3/16'' from the edge of each leg and adjust the depth of cut for a full 1/16''. I use start and stop reference marks on the router table. Be sure to check your set up with trial cuts before making the long cuts on each leg. You can use knife and a small chisel or a Dremel router or both to make the short cuts. It will be necessary to square up the corners of the slots with a knife and a small chisel.

It is also possible to prepare an inlaying template guide for the legs which can be used with a portable router. This

kind of jig would allow you to duplicate the same inlay pattern time and time again. A jig such as this is explained in the chapter *Router Fixture Design*.

The bell flower inlays should be prepared next. The flower design should be drawn full size on a piece of paper. Later this drawing will be cemented to the veneer. You will need two each of three different size flowers. Begin by gluing three or four pieces of curly maple or holly veneer together with a sheet of typing paper between each ply. Actually only two plys of veneer are needed, but with three or four you will have some to choose from. Polyvinyl glue can be used for this operation. After at least an overnight drying period, the veneer sandwich can be removed from clamps. Next glue the full size flower pattern to the surface of the veneer. Now cut the flowers from the sandwich with a jeweler's saw or a precision jig saw. The edges of the flower shapes can be smoothed by carefully filing and sanding. The individual flowers can now be split from the sandwich by laying a knife blade on the paper joint and slicing them off.

Now carefully locate the flowers on the centerline of each leg. Mark around each flower with a sharp pencil or a knife point. The wood under each flower can be cut away using a knife and chisel, however, I usually use a Dremel tool with a router base and a dental burr. The flowers should be inlaid so the surface of the veneer is flush with the leg surface or slightly above.

The small 1/28'' lines between each flower should be cut next before the flowers are glued in place. I cut these lines with a knife and small chisel. I made a small inlaying chisel for this purpose with a 1/28'' cutting edge out of an old 1/8'' twist drill shank. It is important to make these slots just wide enough for your 1/28'' veneer and approximately 1/16'' deep.

The bell flowers can be glued in with a polyvinyl glue. It is usually best to apply light clamping pressure to the flowers when gluing. It is important to let the glue in the inlay assembly dry completely before sanding the surface. Moisture from the glue expands the veneers and premature sanding can result in a slightly sunken inlay later.

The 1/16'' x 1/16'' inlay strips are very difficult to buy nowadays. Many places sell 1/28'' x 1/16'' strips which I really do not like to work with. We started making our own inlay strips several years ago using the following procedure.

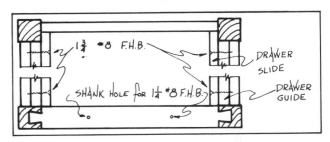

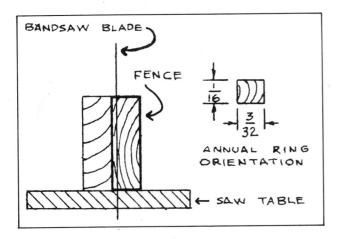

Surface a maple or holly board approximately ¾'' x 2'' x 24'' and edge both edges. Next, use a bandsaw to resaw strips from the blank which are 3/32'' thick. It is important to consider the grain orientation and possible ray fleck problems in making this resaw cut. It is best to orient the cuts so an approximate tangential (flat sawn) surface shows on the front of each 1/16'' strip to avoid distracting ray fleck.

After resawing the strips from each surface of the board, surface the piece again and saw off two more strips. I usually go ahead and make several inlay strip blanks for future use while I am into this operation.

The next job involves accurately ripping the 3/32'' pieces into 1/16'' wide strips. You can use a small 4'' Dremel table saw with a sharp crosscut blade and a specially modified (close fitting) throat plate for this operation. I have used the Dremel saw successfully but most of the time I use a small homemade table saw for this purpose. It is important in this operation to check the inlay width carefully in the inlay slots to be sure of a nice fit. Once the width has been established all of the strips can be ripped. The strips will now have three good edges and one bandsaw rough edge. When gluing them in the inlay slots the bandsaw rough surface is up to be sanded off later.

The inlay strips can now be cut to length and fitted to the slots. Cut them with a sharp knife or chisel mitering each

corner. It may be necessary to moisten the curved inlay pieces or they could be bent over a hot pipe. It is probably best to glue each inlay strip in as soon as it is fitted. Apply a small bead of glue to the slot, not the inlay, and press the strip in place. Roll the strips down to be sure they have bottomed out in the slots. The inlaid surfaces can be sanded after the glue has dried overnight.

After leg inlaying is complete the table aprons and rails can be prepared and joints can be made. It is important to sand the outside surface of the side and back aprons before they are assembled. The leg, apron, rail assembly can be glued after sanding.

Drawer and drawer slide/guide construction is next. I prefer to hand cut the drawer dovetail when time permits but router cut dovetails could also be used. The drawer front is inlaid using the same techniques described for the legs. The drawer slides and guides are secured to the side aprons with glue and screws.

The top is prepared last. Attach the top to the side and back aprons with metal table top clips and screws which allow for expansion. Two 1¼'' #8 flat head screws are used to fasten the top to the top front rail.

Sand all exterior surfaces through 220 grit before finishing. I have finished these tables in several different ways. The technique I like best simply involves applying several thin coats of lacquer sealer and lacquer with heavy 400 grit sanding between coats, letting the lacquer slowly fill the mahogany pores. I continue this lacquer/sand process until the pores are filled. This technique does not color the inlay or darken the mahogany and leaves the wood color as natural as it can be, but it is slow. A Brown paste filler could be used after a thin sealer coat to speed the filling of the pores. The sealer coat will protect the inlay from the color of the filler. Sealer and lacquer top coats can then be sprayed over the dried filler.

Finally, after the last coat of lacquer has dried several days, sand it with 400 grit paper and then buff the entire table with 0000 steel wool to produce a satin sheen.

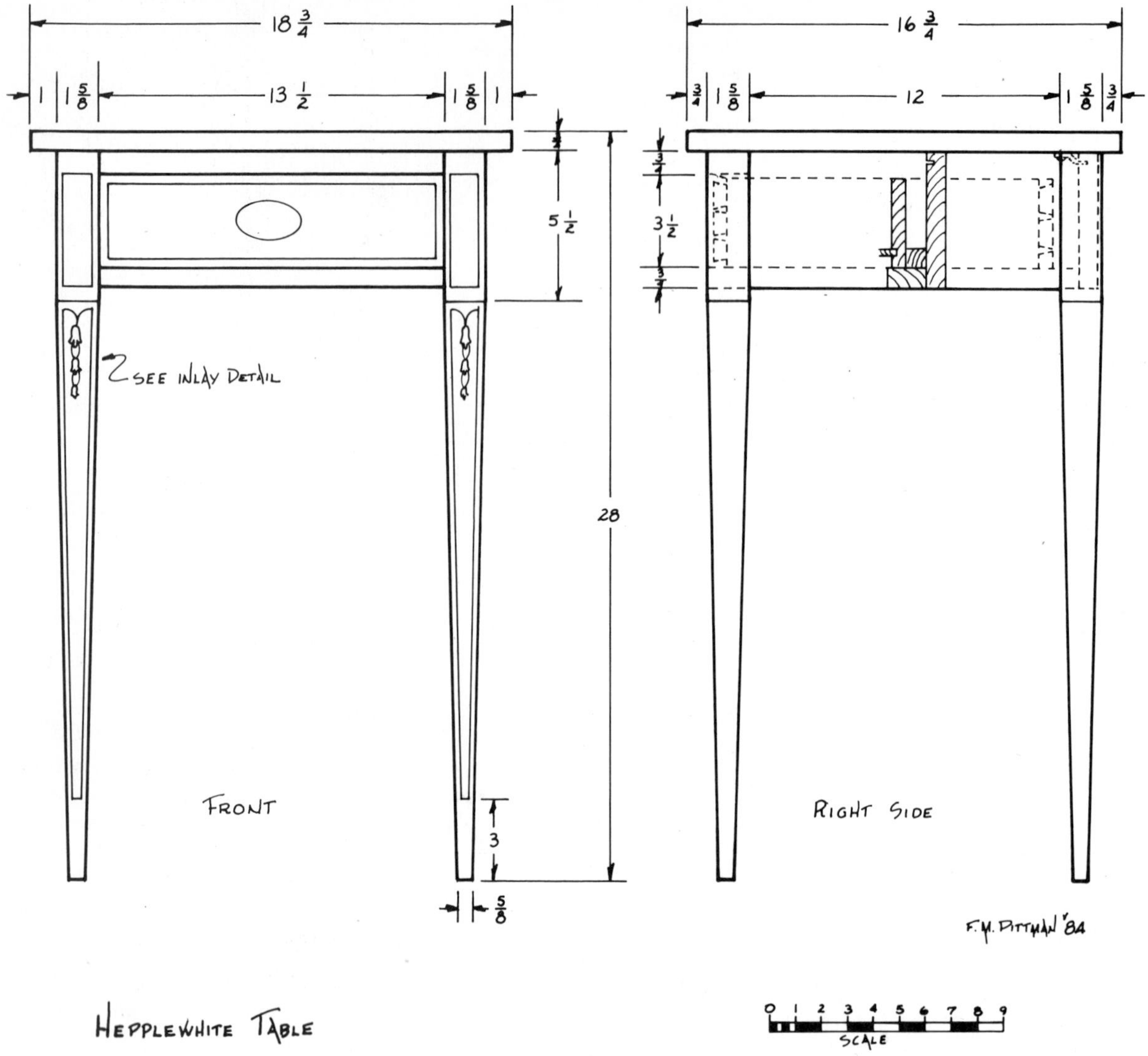
18 3/4
1
1 5/8
13 1/2
1 5/8
1
5 1/2
28
SEE INLAY DETAIL
FRONT
3
5/8
16 3/4
3/4
1 5/8
12
1 5/8
3/4
3 1/2
RIGHT SIDE
F.M. PITTMAN '84
0 1 2 3 4 5 6 7 8 9
SCALE

HEPPLEWHITE TABLE

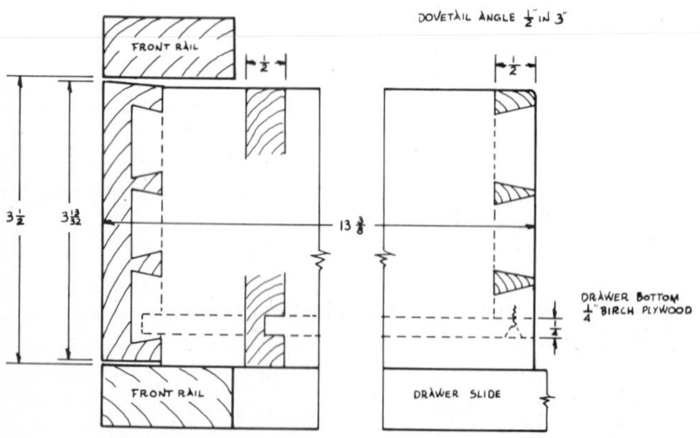
FRONT RAIL
DOVETAIL ANGLE 1/2" IN 3"
1/2
1/2
3 1/2
3 13/32
13 3/8
DRAWER BOTTOM
1/4" BIRCH PLYWOOD
FRONT RAIL
DRAWER SLIDE
0 1 2 3
SCALE

DRAWER DETAIL

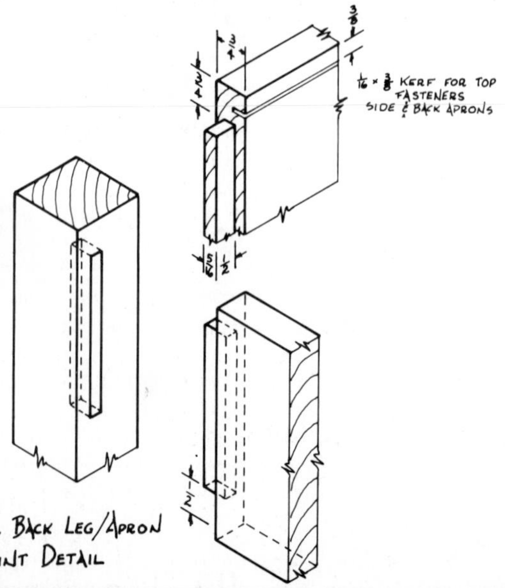
3/8
3/4
1/16 × 3/8 KERF FOR TOP FASTENERS SIDE & BACK APRONS
1/2
5/16

TYPICAL BACK LEG/APRON JOINT DETAIL

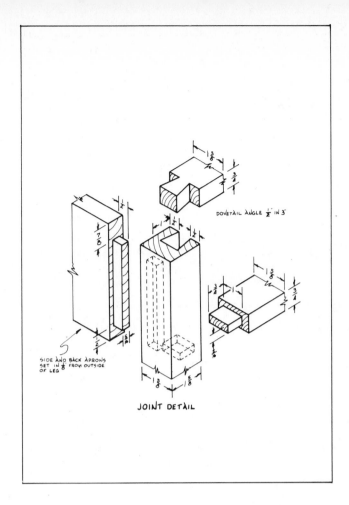

SIDE AND BACK APRONS
SET IN ⅛ FROM OUTSIDE
OF LEG

DOVETAIL ANGLE ½ IN 3

JOINT DETAIL

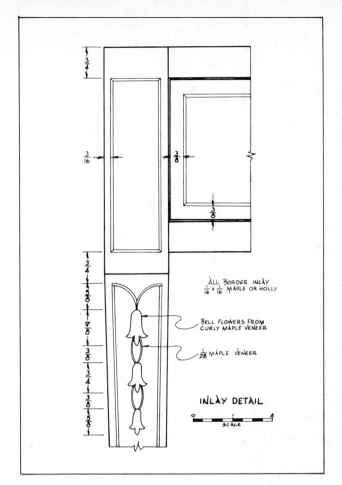

ALL BORDER INLAY
1/16 x 1/16 MAPLE OR HOLLY

BELL FLOWERS FROM
CURLY MAPLE VENEER

1/28 MAPLE VENEER

INLAY DETAIL

SCALE

BILL OF MATERIALS

Quantity	Description	Wood	Dimensions T x W x L
1	Top	Mahogany	¾ x 16 ¾ x 18 ¾
4	Legs	Mahogany	1 5/8 x 1 5/8 x 27 ¼
2	Side Aprons	Mahogany	¾ x 5 x 13
1	Back Apron	Mahogany	¾ x 5 x 14 ½
1	Top Front Rail	Mahogany	¾ x 1 5/8 x 15 ½
1	Lower Front Rail	Mahogany	¾ x 1 5/8 x 15
1	Drawer Front	Mahogany	¾ x 3 13/32 x 13 13/32
2	Drawer Sides	Poplar	½ x 3 13/32 x 13 1/8
1	Drawer Back	Poplar	½ x 3 5/16 x 13 13/32
1	Drawer Bottom	Birch Plywood	¼ x 12 29/32 x 12 7/8
2	Drawer Slide	Poplar	¾ x 1 ½ x 12 ¾
2	Drawer Guide	Poplar	¾ x ¾ x 12
2	Drawer Stop	Poplar	¾ x ¾ x 7/8

Inlay:
1/16 x 1/16 Holly or Maple, approximately 150 inches.
1/28 Maple veneer, approximately eight square inches.

Hardware:
Drawer pull, antique brass oval, 2" bore, back plate approximately 1 ¾ x 2 5/8 similar to D-37 or D-35 from Ball and Ball.

Table top clips . . . . 6 each
Wood screws #8, 5/8" Round head . . . . 6 each
Wood screws #8, 1¼ " Flat head . . . . . . 2 each
Wood screws #8, 1¾ " Flat head . . . . . . 4 each

FRANK PITTMAN is the Graphic Drawing Editor for **The American Woodworker.**

Router Fixture Design

A DEVICE FOR INLAYING A HEPPLEWHITE TABLE LEG

By J. H. Lyons

JIG IN THE UPRIGHT POSITION.

Design Problems and Limitations:

The fixture shown is designed for use with a portable electric hand router used for inlaying the "Hepplewhite" table legs shown on page 20. This fixture locks the legs in position so the router can be manipulated to cut the rectangular grooves necessary for inlaying. The fixture itself, although simple in design, is a third generation of ideas. Several elements were tested as the design process began and the final product resulted in an accurate quality fixture with minimum of set-up time and use.

One hurdle in designing was the difficulty of tapering the leg to achieve precision dimensions each time. Because the groove is positioned so close to the edges of the leg, any slight deviation in making the leg to its necessary dimensions would appear magnified after the inlay is glued and sanded. To overcome this problem, the leg *must* be positioned in the fixture using light center lines drawn on the leg near the end of each inlay area. Using these center lines, you then register them to the permanent center lines located on the fixture itself. So, laying out accurate center lines are a must for this operation. Underneath the fixture is attached the only standard "locator" as it registers the leg in its length dimension. The piece is made of wood and screwed on from the top.

A second design element was to make the fixture base itself as thin as possible (so you would have enough depth of cut) and allow a very flat stable surface to pull the wood of the leg up against (one-quarter inch thick aluminum serves to meet these specifications). As above, this fixture only works as accurately as you make the leg i.e., the surface of the wood you choose to inlay must be perfectly flat. If there are any low areas along the length of the taper, the router bit will not cut enough "depth" since the router always rides on the top of the fixture surface.

Design Concept and Construction:

As the photos show, the basic fixture design is simple. The outside dimensions of the aluminum sheet I used are not magic, but just happen to be the size of the aluminum I had access to. Also, the wooden ends are not critical in shape or size but should allow enough working room underneath for your hands to operate the locking clamps. Notice that both wooden ends do have a square slot in them so you may slide the leg into the fixture from the ends. The wood "step" that flares out from the ends allows you to set the fixture on a typical work bench and temporarily clamp it down while using the fixture. What is critical, of course, is the layout of the taper and square area on the top surface of the aluminum. Using layout dye and a sharp awl, scratch the surface for these areas. To make the cut-outs, I used a bandsaw to internally cut them as close as possible and then hand filed and sanded. There are several other possible ways to make these cuts. Center lines should now be nicked into the aluminum with a small rectangular file.

Basic Fixture Use:

- Secure the necessary parts as indicated for the router.
- Lock in the leg into the desired area to be grooved. Align center lines and lock with clamps.
- Adjust the depth of cut of the bit so the groove is a bit less than 1/16 inch deep.
- Allow any area of the router base to ride on the top surface of the aluminum while tilting the router up. What you are going to do is to establish the "feel" for balance as you let the very tip of the router bushing rest

BOTTOM VIEW OF THE JIG.

just inside the cutouts. After you get your balance, turn the router on and do the same thing but this time gradually let the tip of the bushing move very slowly down the edge of the cutout and then into the wood to start the cut. Be very deliberate and work carefully and slowly so the router bit does not come in contact with the aluminum fixture.

• You will continue lowering the tilt of the router until the router base is flat against the surface of the aluminum.

• Once entering the cut, move slowly around the inside of the cutout allowing the router bushing to guide itself against the cutout at all times. Do not slip.

• When you reach the end of the cut, turn off the router with one hand while holding it with the other. Wait until the bit stops before removing from the cut.

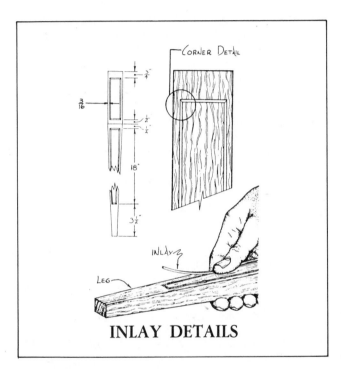

INLAY DETAILS

tional inlays such as "bell flowers" may be used on this leg to more completely detail the original. These inlays are more or less hand-crafted and handfitted into grooves rather than mechanical operations such as the fixture described here. Refer to the drawing for exact dimensions of the inlay location.

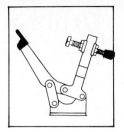

TYPICAL CLAMP

Installation of Inlay:
• The grooves of the leg should be cleaned out with a small chisel or sanded to get the fuzz and burrs off.

• Using a chisel, square up the slightly rounded outside corners of the groove.

• Using a strip of inlay, trial fit into the groove (note: the inlay pieces themselves were made using a small four inch dremel saw). The inlay should fit snugly.

• Place a square end into one corner and draw a straight line from the outside corner to the inside corner of the groove across the inlay itself. This should represent a 45 degree angle.

• Pull the inlay from the groove, place on a scrap block and use a hand chisel to chop straight down across the pencil line. Place back in groove corner to check alignment. Then proceed to the other end of inlay, mark, and cut miter. The piece should now fit into the length of the one groove you've been working with. Pull out inlay once again if everything fits, run a small bead of glue in the groove and immediately insert the inlay back in. You may roll or lightly tap it in and should expect some moderate "squeeze-out."

• Take a square chisel or scraper and scrape off all excess glue before proceeding.

• You then simply work around each groove until you have the inlay in, and each corner will represent a "mitre joint."

• After overnight glue drying, sand the leg surface to your satisfaction.

"INLAYING THE HEPPLEWHITE LEG"
Suggestion for Preparing the Leg:
Depending upon the kinds of machines, equipment and hand tools you have available, here are a couple of different approaches to make the leg.
A. For Limited Machine and Hand Tools:
• Prepare the rectangular blank to dimensions (1 5/8 x 1 5/8 x 27 1/4)
• Lay off the taper according to dimensions.
• Bandsaw the excess material away. The closer and straighter you perform this operation, the less work you have to do in subsequent operations.
• Hand plane, joint, or edge sand to accurate size.
• Now ready for use in the fixture.
B. For Machine use Only:
• Use a tapering jig on the table saw to rip the tapers. Exercise caution because this operation should be conducted with an assistant or helper since it is dangerous.
• Jointing or edge sanding and/or hand sanding may be done at this time.
• Now ready for use in the fixture.
Locations of the Inlay:
The actual location of the inlay is near the same as the original design that George Hepplewhite used in making these tables back in the late 1700's. The use of tapers and inlays are famous trade-marks of the Hepplewhite era. Addi-

TABLES
USING PRODUCTION FRAMES
by Frederick Wilbur

As has been pointed out in numerous articles recently, the sole proprietor woodworker tends to be more efficient if he/she can design for a limited production item, as opposed to the strictly one of a kind. In so doing, the one of a kind quality remains, but the unit price is competitive. I designed the tables presented here with this concept in mind. The basic *structure* of the piece is easily mass produced, but the aesthetic or decorative details are numerous and can be varied easily. I will begin by describing the basic coffee table shown in the picture and in the drawings.

I thought that the box frame for the legs allowed the most possibilities, so I made two square units using 1 x 4 red oak. The joint is a simple finger joint made on a table saw using a straightforward jig (described in Tage Frid's *Teaching Woodworking, Book 1, Joinery,* p. 90).

By using this joint all the frame members are of the same width and length, simplifying the cut list. The width of the frame members need not be 4 inches, but the finger width should be in proportion to the thickness of the material. Alone, this joint is not strong enough to resist lateral pressure so a stabilizing brace of some sort is necessary. I let-in a piece of oak into the sides of the frame and fastened the piece to the top frame member allowing the piece to ride in dovetailed notches. This structural brace became, at least in this piece, the background for the decorative drops. I cut an uplifting arch from the brace to lighten the feeling of the piece and to create a balance with the trio of drops. This completes the basic supporting unit to which we now add a top and decoration.

I next turned the six drops of walnut by eye, the slight variations lending a comfortable subtlety to the piece. I matched the turnings and installed them in regularly spaced fashion. I chose to turn drops but the turnings could have extended down to the base of the frame. Note the variations in the drawings. In any event, any number of these turnings would not replace the stability afforded by the let-in brace.

I used a piece of walnut for the top because I thought that the continuity of color into the decorative turnings would add more interest in the piece. Not only does the flat utilitarian top surface continue mysteriously below itself in the drops, but the decorative aspect of the drops draws attention to itself, therefore minimizing the emphasis on structure. Using all one species of wood, especially a light colored wood, would be much subtler and to some, no doubt, more sophisticated. I used a large # 7 gouge to relieve the under three inches of the table top ends leaving the gouge marks to render a scalloped edge.

Assembling the leg units is quickly accomplished. Fixing the top slab to the leg units was, admittedly, a little more involved on this particular table than need be. I had

turned the drops with a "collar" and a dowel-like projection in order to use them as the connection between frame and top. The middle drop was inserted into the top of the frame, glued and wedged. I then cut it flush with the frame member. The two other drops extended through slots in the frame and into holes drilled in the top. I glued and wedged these. Production considerations would demand that all three drops end at the frame, and that the leg unit be screwed (in slots) to the top.

After this successful piece, I took a few minutes to explore the variations on the theme, and I came up with a range of furniture types which could use this same idea. I have made another table which carried the finger jointed box concept just one step further. The bedside table is now made of rectangular frames. The bracing panel is now a pierced carving. The sides of the frame

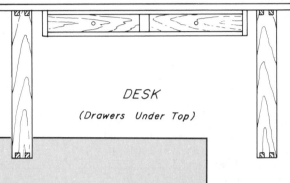

DESK
(Drawers Under Top)

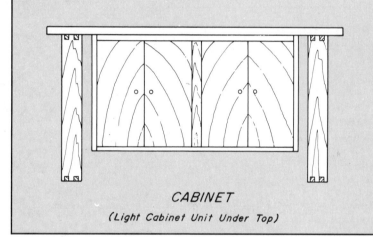

CABINET
(Light Cabinet Unit Under Top)

members do not need to be the same width all along their length so I thinned the bottom stretcher. I also incorporated a slatted shelf. Again, I thought that contrasting woods (red oak and mahogany) would contribute to the aesthetic appeal. The pierced carving and the use of slats for the shelf lighten the effect of the piece.

Several changes in structure should be pointed out between the two tables. The carved panels are inset into the frame sides by sliding dovetails before the top frame member is glued in place. A groove in this frame member allows for the expansion, if any, of the carved panel. The slatted shelf could be made of a solid piece for necessary bracing of the legs on a larger piece. I screwed the frame to the top using four screws per unit placed on alternate sides of the frame member for maximum bearing.

I think that you can begin to see the possibilities of this design, both as a mass produced piece and as a customized product. This sort of structure lends itself to more sophisticated pieces such as desks, (by hanging drawers under the top as illustrated in the sketches) or as a sideboard. This simple modular leg assembly can accommodate endless variations.

Turnings

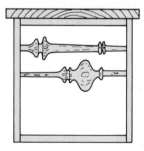

Turnings

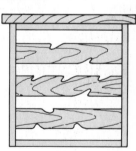

Slats

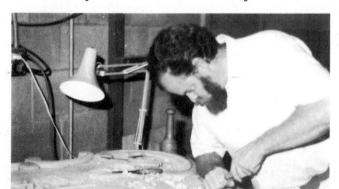

ABOUT THE AUTHOR
Frederick Wilbur is a professional woodworker specializing in carving.

27

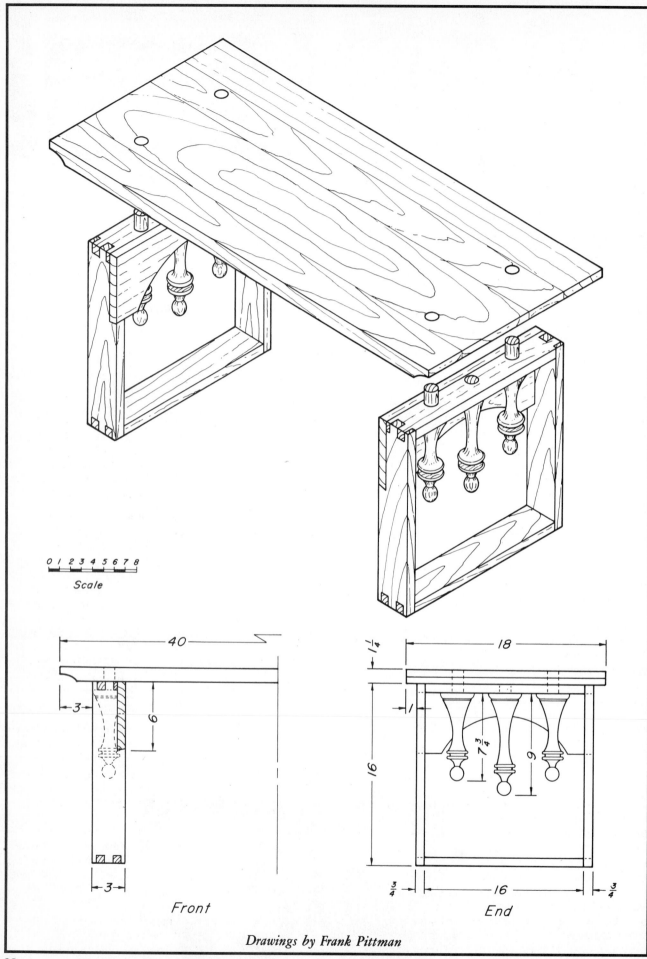

0 1 2 3 4 5 6 7 8
Scale

40

3

6

3

Front

1 1/4

18

1

16

7 3/4

9

3/4   16   3/4

End

Drawings by Frank Pittman

PHOTOGRAPHS BY THE AUTHOR

This end table illustrates how dowels can be used to make strong joints. By exposing the dowels and arranging them in threes the dowels also add a decorative touch.

Doweled End Table

by W. Curtis Johnson

Doweling is perhaps the easiest way to make a joint. Dowels may be purchased ready made in defined sizes and the worker need only drill matching holes in the two pieces of wood to be joined. Only basic skills and tools are necessary. There is no need for accurate sawing; no need to plane to fit. However, doweling normally suffers from serious deficiencies. It is usually more difficult than seems reasonable to line up the matching holes for the joint. Even with a number of dowels at each joint the amount of gluing surface is minimal. When the dowels are across the grain, roughly half of the gluing surface is to end grain, which has no strength. Furthermore, the seasonal shrink and swell with humidity soon destroys the marginal bond for the remainder of the dowel because this is cross-grain construction. This end table demonstrates how to use dowels to advantage; for

accuracy, structural strength, and decoration.

You will undoubtedly have to glue up some boards to get wide enough pieces for the top, sides, and back. I used 8/4 lumber for the sides and back, resawing them for bookmatching. After resawing I waited two weeks for the lumber to equilibrate before continuing the project. If you don't have a band saw, bookmatching is certainly not mandatory. Indeed, for years I have had a spectacular 4/4 board around that seemed just perfect for this top, so the top isn't bookmatched here. However, I did carefully match the colors at the joint. Remember that the grain of the drawer face should be matched with the grain of the rails.

Begin by enlarging the accompanying patterns as this will make it easy to lay out the required pieces on your lumber. The legs can be interlocked and the layout worked around the inevitable knots. The front has exactly the same shape as the back, but instead of a single glued up board, the front has a number of pieces with grain running in both directions. Still, the design allows for changes in humidity with only the usual short joints involving cross-grain construction.

Cut out all the pieces, and then start assembly by gluing together the sides and back. Plane the joints carefully and dry clamp the pieces before gluing to be sure the joints will be perfect. Check to see that the width at the legs is the same as the width at the top. With the dowel construction it is not necessary to have dados for the drawer runners and rabbets for the kickers, but these grooves make it much easier to align the components. Make the grooves and stop them at the inside edge of the front and back.

To be able to glue the runners and kickers and still avoid cross-grain construction, I run the grain over the width of these pieces instead of along their length. A stretcher is added in the middle between each pair of runners or kickers forming an "H" to prevent the sides of the table from warping and pinching the drawer. Again, you will have to glue up some material. Cut the drawer face and the top and bottom rails for the front to a length that is 1/32″ less than the width of the back. This slightly trapezoidal shape is meant to prevent the drawer from sticking with changes in humidity. Dry clamp

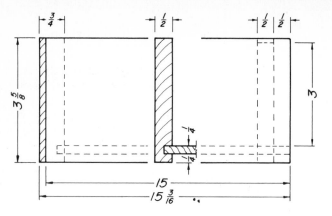

Drawer Detail

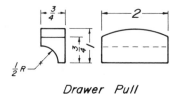

Drawer Pull

2. *The sides and back of the table are bookmatched boards resawed from 8/4 lumber. The dowels in the sides provide simple joints that are important to the structural integrity of the table. The doweled joints are strong because they go into the end grain of the inside board and the square head gives mechanical strength at the outside board.*

at the appropriate places. I like a pattern of threes with the dowels 1″ apart. Use a ¼″ chisel to carefully square up the holes just at the very top. This is also a good time to add the decorative dowels to the back and the drawer face.

The dowels themselves will be round with a square top, and you will have to make these specialty items yourself. First make ¼″x ¼″ strips. It can be dangerous to work with such small pieces of wood if you don't take the proper safety precautions, so be sure to use hold downs and push sticks. Cut the strips into 2¼″ pieces and bevel one end. You will ultimately need 54 dowels. It is a good idea to make extras. The dowel is rounded over 1½″ of its length by pounding it through a ¼″ hole drilled in a piece of steel. Dowel formers of this type are available from most of the mail order houses. You can easily make your own but the dowel needs at least one groove along its rounded length to allow excess glue to escape. Clean up the dowels you have made, put a little glue in each hole with a small brush, and pound each dowel home. Hold the squared end of the dowel with a pair of pliers to keep the end lined up with the squared hole. The dowels tend to twist as they are driven.

Note that this type of doweling avoids all of the deficiencies enumerated at the beginning of this article. The ends of the dowels are exposed so there is no need to predrill holes that would ultimately have to line up. Wherever the dowel is important to structure, the grain in the dowel and the inside piece of wood are parallel, so the glue joint will be strong and unaffected by humidity. There is still cross-grain construction with the outside piece of wood, but the

the carcase together and if everything checks out, round the edges where appropriate and give all the pieces their final smoothing or sanding. Make sure that the width of the top rail is identical to the thickness of the kickers so the drawer will slide properly.

Gluing begins by attaching the runner and kicker assemblies to one side. Follow this by gluing the back to the same side, 1/8″ in from the edge. Now the second side can be glued to the two assemblies and the back. Finally, the top and bottom rails for the front can be glued in place, again 1/8″ in from the edge. Slide in the drawer face edgewise to space the two rails. There should be no play between the drawer face and the rails (or the drawer face and the sides) at this time.

All the end-grain glue joints are now strengthened with dowels. Simply drill ¼″ holes that are 2″ long in the sides

3. *Bookmatching is not mandatory. The top is glued up from a 4/4 board with spectacular grain.*

Dowels are used to join the drawer sides to the face. The simple construction has the sheer strength necessary for a strong joint.

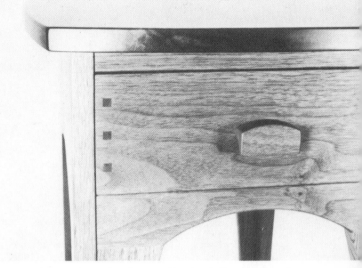

Grain is matched at the drawer. The dowels here are purely decorative and have their counterpart on the back of the table.

square head on the dowel gives mechanical strength. The dowels are used in clusters to provide adequate strength.

The ends of the dowels can be sawed off with a small saw that has no set to its teeth. Cut the dowels to the surface of the sides with a finger plane and sand as necessary. Glue on the front legs with the 1/8″ overhang from the sides. Complete the carcase by drilling the holes for the screws that will attach the top. Elongate the holes to compensate for movement.

After this somewhat demanding work, it is fun to return to an easy job and complete the top. Trim the top to size keeping the glue line in the center. Smooth it and round the edges. Mark for the holes to attach the top to the carcase, and drill angled holes on the inside that you are certain will stop about ¼″ from the top surface. You can wrap masking tape around the drill to mark the depth.

Now it's time to construct the drawer. Make a ½″ rabbet 9/16″ deep for the sides in the inside ends of the drawer face. This will remove parts of the dowels with the decorative ends. Cut a ¼″ × ¼″ groove along the inside of the drawer face and the sides for the drawer bottom. Cut a ½″ wide by ¼″ deep dado across the insides of the sides for the back of the drawer. Glue the sides to the drawer face and the drawer back in its dado. The bottom of the back should be even with the top of the grooves for the bottom. The joint at the drawer face must resist a lot of abuse as the drawer is slid in and out, and the end grain joint we have now could not be less suitable. However, by placing three dowels through each side and into the face, we obtain a proper joint with strength against the sheer forces of opening a drawer. It is a very simple way to make a very strong drawer. Cut and slide in the bottom and secure it to the back with two small screws. The drawer is now complete but it must be fitted to the carcase.

The drawer should be a very tight fit both horizontally and vertically if it goes into the carcase at all. Plane off the top of the drawer at the face and sides to introduce just 1/32″ of play. Test each corner of the drawer in its proper position (the drawer will have to be upside down when testing the front) and be very careful. It is very easy to remove too much material. Next, plane the sides. There should be no play at all when the back enters the carcase and no more than 1/32″ at the front. Remember that the

carcase has a trapezoidal shape and now we are making the drawer trapezoidal. If all goes according to plan the drawer will slide smoothly but bind a few inches before it releases completely. Glue some stops at the back of the runners to position the drawer correctly when it is all the way in.

We still have the wooden drawer pull to fabricate. Clamp together two 4/4 blocks that are 3″ long and 3″ wide. Drill a 1″ hole in the center of this sandwich along the grain. Separate the two pieces and rip each block along the center of the semicircular groove. This provides the material from which to fashion the drawer pull and enough material left over for three future pulls. Drill the holes for the pull.

This completes basic construction of the end table. The pull is attached to the drawer and the top to the carcase after applying your finish. Now steam out inadvertent dents, do any final sanding, and apply your finish. Finish only the front face of the drawer and don't finish the runners or the kickers. Rub paraffin on the runners and the bottom edges of the drawer for smooth sliding. If you smoothed the pieces before assembly when this task was easier, much of the finishing work is already done.

BILL OF MATERIAL

CODE	NAME	NO. REQ.	T	x	W	x	L
A	Top	1	¾		15¾		22¼
B	Sides	2	¾		18¾		18¾
C	Back	1	¾		11		18¾
D	Top Front Rail	1	¾		¾		10 31/32
E	Lower Front Rail	1	¾		1 7/8		10 31/32
F	Front Leg	2	¾		2 3/8		12½
G	Center Rails	2	¾		1½		11½
H	Kicker Rails	4	¾		7¾		1¾
I	Drawer Slides	4	¾		7¾		1¾
J	Drawer Front	1	¾		3 5/8		10 15/16
K	Drawer Sides	2	½		3 5/8		15
L	Drawer Back	1	½		3		10 7/16
M	Drawer Bottom	1	¼		14 11/16		10 7/16

ABOUT THE AUTHOR:

W. Curtis Johnson is a contributing editor to **The American Woodworker.**

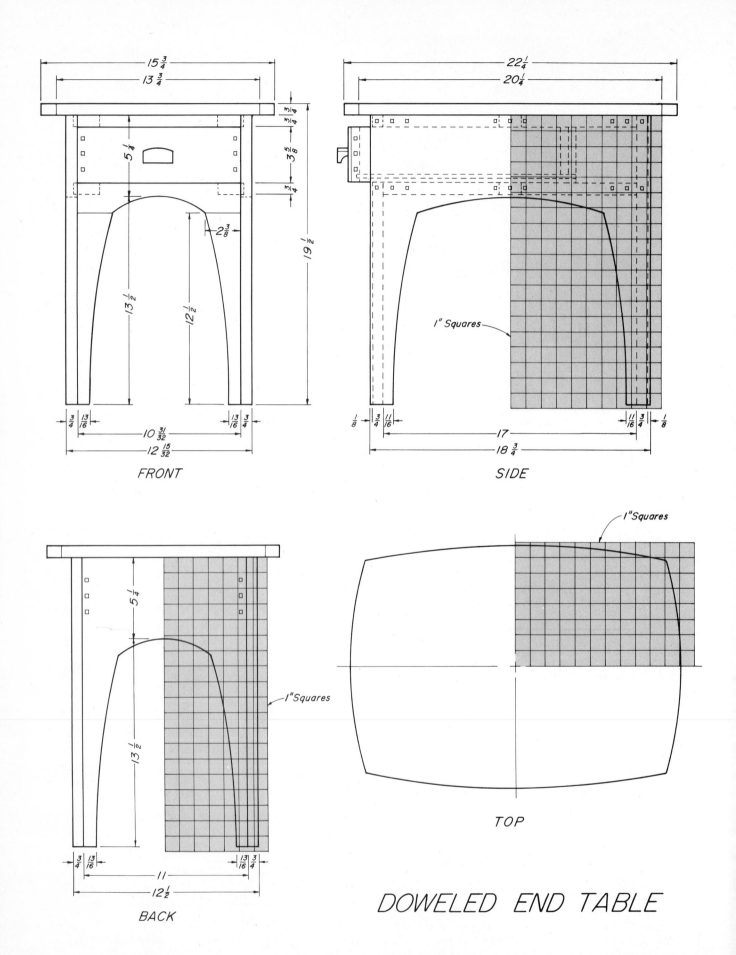

FRONT

SIDE

1" Squares

BACK

1" Squares

TOP

1" Squares

DOWELED END TABLE

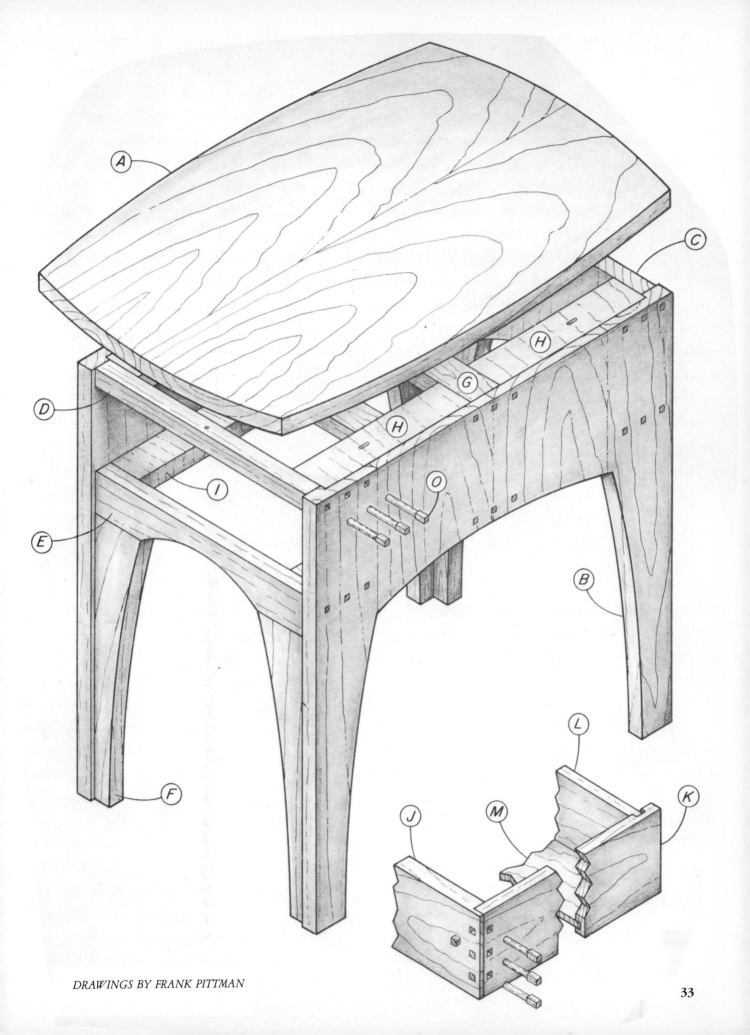

DRAWINGS BY FRANK PITTMAN

BIRDSEYE BEDSIDE TABLE

by Pat Warner

I designed this bedside table of birdseye and hardrock maple for a client who simply couldn't get what she wanted in a furniture store. It stands 26″ high and the top measures 25¼″ x 18¼″. There is no splay to the legs though there is an outside taper. The two radii and taper on these constant thickness legs were router/template cut and dress sanded on an edge radius sander.

The legs are secured front to rear by 5½″ wide rails that are tenoned and flushed to the inside of the leg to offer the drawerbox a guide surface and to simplify the joinery of the sub top. The leg rail assemblies are fastened left to right by the split subtop, the tenoned rear back panel rail and the 3″ wide stick under the front of the drawer.

The top is 9/16″ thick, fully rounded on the ends and square front and rear. It is sized to hang over 1/16″ front and rear and 7/8″ on each side. It's held fast to the subtop with sheet metal screws in slotted holes to accommodate its season changes.

The drawer front and back are glue jointed to the sides and no attempt is made to hide the remaining exposed side panel end grain. Rather, it was sanded to #400 grit and polished to become a design element to highlight the excessive end grain pronounced in the pull. The ¼" birch ply drawer bottom is sized to net the opening of the drawer box plus 3/8". A ¼" x 3/16" groove is formed all around the drawer and then the bottom is glued into this slot. This makes registration easy and helps to square up the box. The box rides on waxed maple runners, ¾" sq., screwed to the rails which are hidden in the front elevation by the stick under the drawer.

The drawer being flush inset must be dimensioned for a good fit lest it rattle and jam on opening and closing. I shoot for the opening minus 1/32" in height and width. Since there is no front to rear seasonal change in the stand, I size the drawer so the rear back panel rail stops the box flush with the front of the subtop.

...designed for a client who couldn't get what she wanted in a furniture store...

The split subtops (2-6" wide x 7/8" thick pieces of hardrock) are glue jointed directly across the leg rail junction flush to the front and rear. Only the most outward 3" of the subtops are glued because there would otherwise be too much cross grain gluing. Blind dovetailing or perhaps splining would be suitable joining alternatives.

The 3" x 7/8" stick under the drawer is also jointed across the legrail junction, but it is tenoned and glued full width. The drawer guides hold the dawer 1/64" over this rail so it offers no slide resistance. The curve was template routed on edge, but careful band sawing could yield the curve as well.

Bill of Material

Part	Description	#Req'd	T	W	L
A	Top	1	9/16	18¼	25¼
B	Sub Top	2	7/8	6	21½
C	Legs	4	1 5/32	1 11/16	25 7/16
D	Side Aprons	2	7/8	5½	17 1/16
E	Rear Apron	1	5/8	5	22½
F	Lower Front Rail	1	7/8	3	22¼
G	Drawer Slide	2	¾	¾	14½
H	Drawer Slide	2	3/8	3 23/32	17¼
I	Drawer Front	1	¾	3 23/32	20½
J	Drawer Bottom	1	¼	16½	20 5/8
K	Drawer Back	1	3/8	3 23/32	20 15/16
L	Drawer Pull	1	¾	7/8	7½

CUTTING LIST INSTRUCTIONS

1. The legs are cut from rectangular section material 1 5/32" x 1 11/16" x 25 7/16". The mortising should be done before any shaping. The mortises (See back leg detail) are ¼" x 5/8" deep from the inside edge for the side rails, and ¼" x ¾" deep, ¼" from the back of the rear legs for the back rail. The bevel at the foot (See Leg Detail) starts 1" from the outside edge of the leg and stops 5/8" up the leg. The long curve runs 10½" up the leg beginning at the bevel. That curve has a constant radius, so if the template is located at the 2 points, the curve will always be the same. The outside cyma and taper can be generated by using Leg Detail Illustration. The leg is narrowest in the cyma as shown in the drawing and tapers out to the outside corners at the floor. All the shaping and mortising were router template cut with flush bearing trimmers. Those skilled on the band saw should have no trouble with these shapes.

2. The rear back panel is 5" x 5/8" and its shoulder to shoulder length is 21". One centered tenon is formed on either end ¾" long with 3/16" shoulders all around.

3. The side panels are 5½" x 7/8" x 15 13/16" shoulder to shoulder. The centered 5/8" long tenons are ¼" thick with 5/16" shoulders.

4. The stick under the drawer starts at 3" x 7/8" x 22¼". It is located below the subtop to produce a 3¾" opening for the drawer. One centered 5/8" long tenon ¼" thick is formed on either end with 5/16" shoulders all around. The curve is actually of constant radius and was generated with a 25 foot string and pencil (the radius is therefore 25 feet). The curve narrows to about a ½" in the center of the stick. It is tenoned across the leg rail joint where its mortise was cut after the leg/rail is glued.

5. The two subtops are 6" x 7/8" thick and are glue jointed across the leg rail joint. They should net 21" (shoulder to shoulder) after glue jointing, dovetailing or tenoning.

6. The drawer height is 3¾" (Less 1/64" - 1/32") and the starting dimensions of sides, front, and back will depend on the method of joinery.

7. The drawer pull, also of birdseye, is fluted top and bottom, 7½" long x ¾" high x 7/8" thick. The end bevels approximate the leg ends.

8. The top is 9/16" x 25¼" x 18¼".

About The Author:
Pat Warner is a designer and furniture maker from Escondido, California.

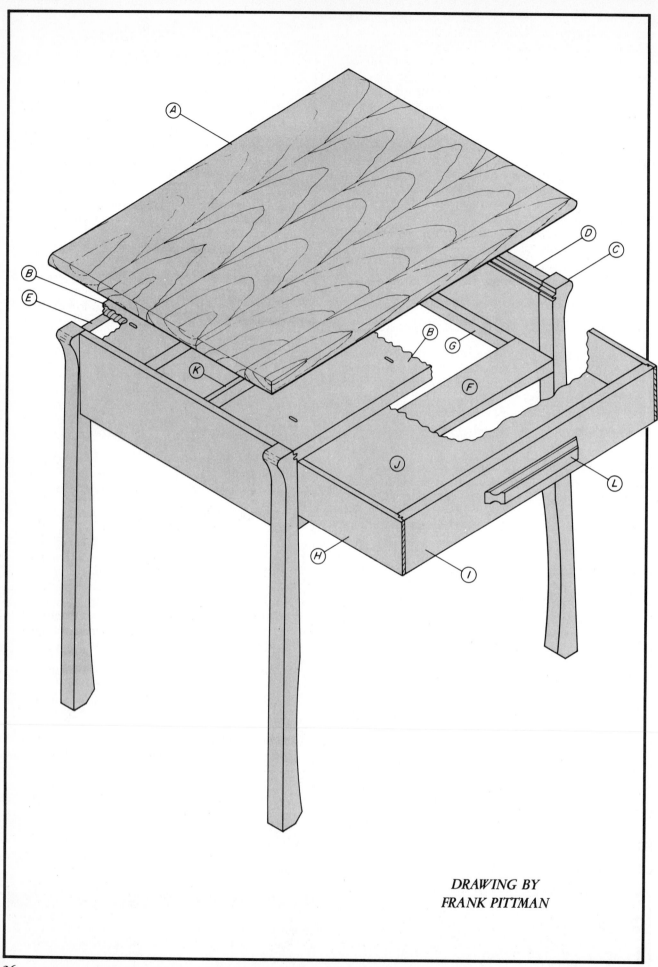

DRAWING BY
FRANK PITTMAN

BEDSIDE TABLE

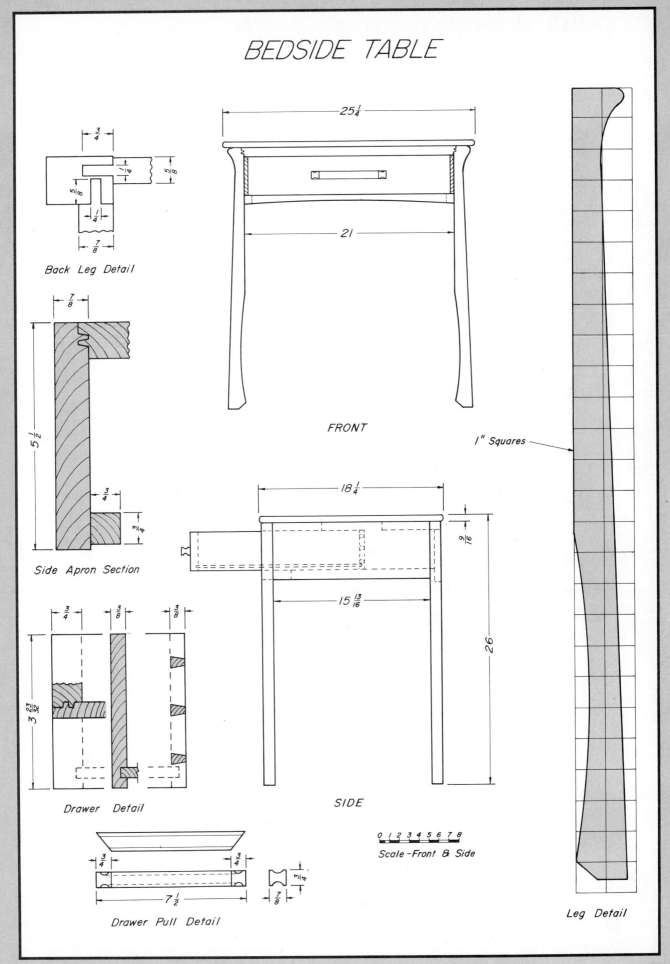

Back Leg Detail

Side Apron Section

Drawer Detail

Drawer Pull Detail

FRONT

SIDE

Scale - Front & Side

1" Squares

Leg Detail

CONTEMPORARY CHAIR

by W. Curtis Johnson

This contemporary chair is styled after the conventional German chairs for a particularly sturdy design, but avoids cross grain construction.

Photographs by the Author

I have always liked the way in which traditional German chairs combine a simple style with an extremely sturdy design. However, their weak point is the cross-grain construction at the seat, which invariably leads to cracking. Recently, I realized that these chairs could be made using the principles in my "Bench-Coffee Table" (*The American Woodworker, Vol. 1, No. 3*) to avoid the design flaw of cross-grain construction. The result is the chair presented here.

Following the methods used in the construction of the Bench-Coffee Table, the legs are made in pairs from a single board and attached to the seat with through mortise and tenon joints. To avoid cross-grain construction, the grain runs across the seat rather than front to back, as is conventional. The seat is strengthened across the grain by the wood joining the two legs. The back goes through the seat to become one of the stretchers strengthening the legs. With this design, the back is attached at two points over five inches apart, so it is particularly sturdy. The legs are angled 5º to the side, and the back continues this line. The legs are angled 7º to the front and back. All in all, I was pleased with the sculptural effect.

I chose fairly standard dimensions for maximizing the comfort of a side chair, as discussed in *Fine Woodworking Magazine, Nos. 14, 16, and 32*. Thus the seat is 17½ inches from the floor at the front and tilts back at 3º. The seat itself is 15 inches deep and 17½ inches wide at the front. This chair was designed for our small kitchen table, so for increased comfort I'd suggest enlarging the width of the seat and the back one inch over the dimensions given here. The angle between the seat and the back is 100º.

Regardless of the wood you choose for your chair, the wide boards will undoubtedly have to be glued up from two narrow ones. I used 8/4 lumber and resawed it on my band saw so that the wide boards are book-matched when glued together. However, you can certainly use standard 4/4 lumber and match the grain at the joints. The Bill of Materials assumes that you will use 4/4 lumber with one-half the width of the wide boards, and pair the pieces for the legs and back to minimize waste. If you use 8/4 lumber and resaw it, the board for the back need be only 26½ inches long, and the waste can be used for stretchers.

Trim and smooth the edges of your lumber, making sure that the edges are square to the faces. Then enlarge all the shapes in the drawing to full size and transcribe them to your boards. Cut the curves with a band saw or a saber saw. However, don't cut the 2 inch radius on the back, since you will need that corner when clamping. Furthermore, the blank for the seat should be rectangular rather than trapezoidal to facilitate accurate measuring if you plan to cut the mortises by hand. Use a variable jig for cutting tapers, as described in *The American Woodworker, Vol.1, No. 2,* to cut the slants at the center of the back and legs. The stretchers should be a little long so they can be adjusted later.

Begin assembly with the back because the finished dimensions of this piece will determine the exact positions of the legs. Plane the 5° slant at the center of the back and the ends which will join the stretcher. Clamp the back together at the top and check this joint. If everything looks good, mark the final length of the stretcher from the assembled back and cut off the excess. The stretcher can't be glued directly to the main part of the back because glue has no strength on end grain. You should use two dowels or a floating tenon at each of these joints. Clamp all three pieces together as a final test before finally gluing up the back. It is a fairly simple matter to plane the 7° slant on the legs and glue them together in pairs. All the curves can now be smoothed, and if you have a drum sander, this process is trivial.

When the seat blank is ready, you can cut the mortises. My method for making wedged mortise and tenon joints by hand was detailed in *The American Woodworker, Vol. 1, No. 3,* although it is a little trickier here because the legs slant out at 5°. However, if your seat blank is carefully squared, you can use an adjustable square to accurately mark out the mortises. The slant means that they must be about 1/16 of an inch closer to the side of the seat on the bottom. Size the width of the mortises about 1/32 of an inch less than the thickness of the leg sections so you can fit the tenon to the mortise. The distance across the top of the seat between the insides of the mortises should be the same as the distance across your finished back at 20½ inches from the top. Clamp a scrap of wood, cut at 85° at the mortise to help you maintain the correct angle with the chisel, and cut from both sides. Of course, the mortises can always be cut with a router fitted

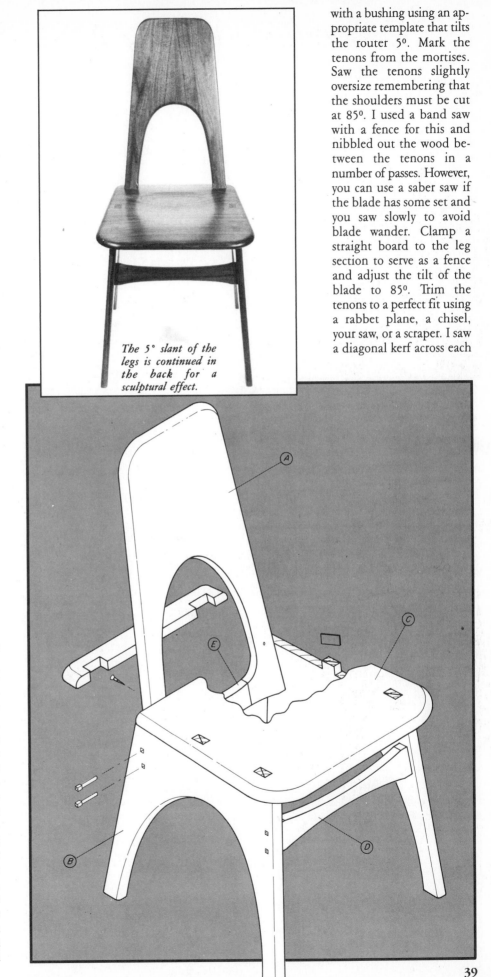

The 5° slant of the legs is continued in the back for a sculptural effect.

with a bushing using an appropriate template that tilts the router 5°. Mark the tenons from the mortises. Saw the tenons slightly oversize remembering that the shoulders must be cut at 85°. I used a band saw with a fence for this and nibbled out the wood between the tenons in a number of passes. However, you can use a saber saw if the blade has some set and you saw slowly to avoid blade wander. Clamp a straight board to the leg section to serve as a fence and adjust the tilt of the blade to 85°. Trim the tenons to a perfect fit using a rabbet plane, a chisel, your saw, or a scraper. I saw a diagonal kerf across each tenon to accept a wedge after assembly. Check the fit with the legs in place, but don't glue them in quite yet.

Customers often ask me how I got the back through the seat, and I've thought of a number of clever answers, but woodworkers will realize at once that the seat was simply cut and reglued. That is your next task. First trim the seat to shape and round the edges to a ¼ inch radius on the bottom and a ½ inch radius on the top. This is also a good time to do any trimming on the legs and back and round over the edges on these sections. The legs and the rear of the back sport a ¼ inch radius, while the front of the back has a ½ inch radius. Be careful not to round the back where it will go through the seat. Now rip the seat to accommodate the back. The cut should be 10° from vertical to give a total angle of 100° between the seat and the back. Plane these edges smooth and check the joint.

Sand all of the pieces except the top of the seat through 220 grit in preparation for assembly. Secure the leg sections by gluing the tenons into their mortises and driving in the wedges along with a little glue. When the glue is dry, trim the protruding ends of the tenons flush to the seat with a plane. Now is the time to hollow out the seat to a depth of about 3/8 inch at the center. Use other comfortable chairs as a model for the hollow. You can rough this out with a gouge, but since I was doing four chairs I made a template for use with a router. The template has four rings to provide five ever larger guides for the outside of the router. With

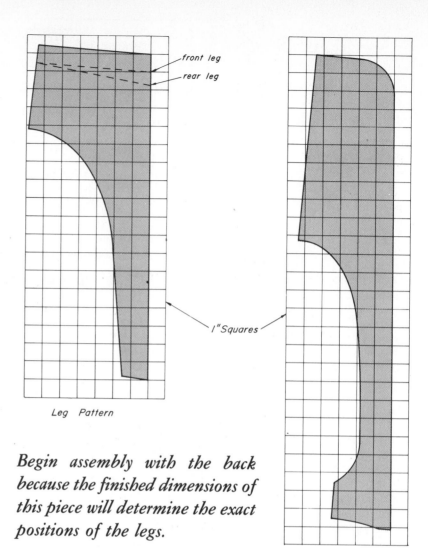

Leg Pattern

Begin assembly with the back because the finished dimensions of this piece will determine the exact positions of the legs.

Back Pattern

The legs are slanted 7° front and back, and the wood between the legs strengthens the seat across the grain. The seat is tilted back 3° and the back angled 100° to the seat.

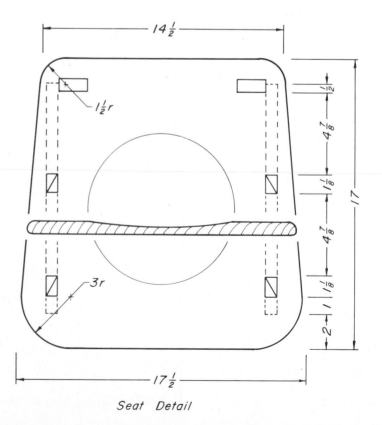

Seat Detail

all the rings in place I rout to 5/32 of an inch. As each ring is removed, I raise the bit 1/32 of an inch, but I don't rout near the back on the fifth pass so that this part of the hollow will be steeper. A flexible disk sander on a drill is excellent for shaping and smoothing.

Now, position the back and drill through the back into the seat for a 2-inch no. 10 wood screw on each side. Glue the back to the seat and the leg sections, holding it in place with the screws and clamping the legs snug against the edges at the bottom of the back. Next, mark the mortises in the remaining seat piece from the back and saw the mortises to fit. Glue the seat together. Mark the length of the front stretcher from the legs and glue this in place.

Exposed dowels secure the front stretcher and strengthen the joint between the back and the legs. You can use commercial round dowels, but I prefer to make my own so they have square tops. I rip ¼ inch square lengths of material and cut the blanks about ¼ inch longer than needed. Then I drive the square pegs through a ¼ inch round hole drilled in a piece of steel, stopping to leave a square top about 3/8 in long. The dowels are cleaned up and the round end chamfered. These dowels will be used in 1/4 inch holes that have plenty of depth and are squared at the top with a chisel. This chair uses two such dowels at either end of the front and rear stretchers. Trim the ends of the dowels flush with the legs after they are glued in place.

Sanding before the chair is assembled and care in using the right amount of glue will mean that very little must be done before applying the finish. Raise any dents with a damp cloth and an iron, and sand where necessary. The finish is your choice.

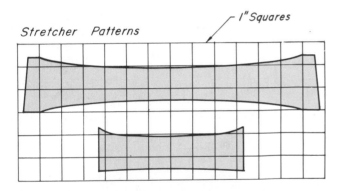

Stretcher Patterns

1" Squares

Bill of Materials

A.	1 Back	3/4" x 6" x 39"
B.	2 Leg sections	3/4" x 7" x 24"
C.	1 Seat	3/4" x 17" x 17 1/2"
D.	1 Front stretcher	3/4" x 2 3/8" x 13 1/2"
E.	1 Rear stretcher	3/4" x 2" x 6 3/4"

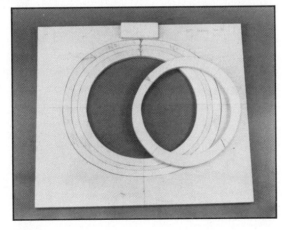

This jig guides the outside of a router when roughing out the hollow in the seat. Four rings provide five guides for depths of 5/32, 1/8, 3/32, 1/16, and 1/32 of an inch.

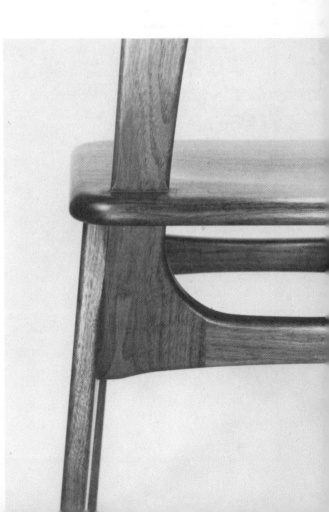

ABOUT THE AUTHOR:
W. Curtis Johnson is a contributing editor to **The American Woodworker.**

CHAIR

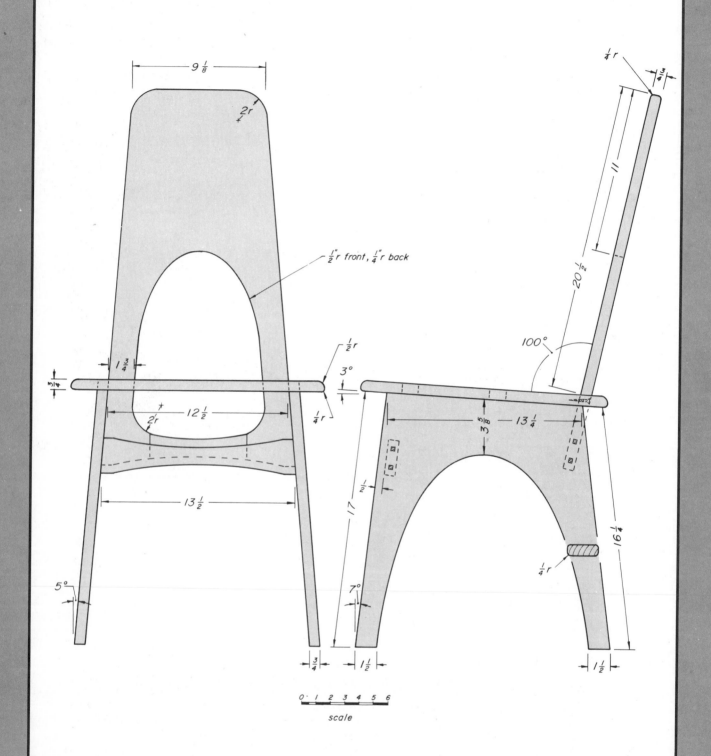

scale

Drawings by Frank Pittman

As rocking chairs became more and more accepted as parlor furniture, the platform rocker became very popular, especially with the middle class. Its invention is credited to Samuel H. Bean from Philadelphia. Noted in his patent of 1840 is the fact that ''his stationary base rocker would do away with the long and cumbersome rockers on the common chair, which occupy a great deal of room and are very destructive to carpets.'' The platform rocker really got moving after 1850 or so. These rockers were very expensive for their time and ranged in price from a plain chair at $26.00 to a fancy model at a cost of $45.00 or more. By 1890 the platform rocker was considered an essential piece of furniture.

I believe this model was made by B.A. Atkinson around 1890 in the Atkinson factory on Washington Street in Boston, Massachusetts.

The platform rocker was mass produced by somewhat crude automatic lathes. As I was measuring the original chair for this article, I found that none of the identical turnings matched each other very closely. Nevertheless, these chairs were built to last. The original has the single, 2½" diameter spring that was used in those days.

I found this particular chair in northern Vermont way back in 1953. It originally had a coarse, stiff leathery seat and back which was in very poor condition. For over 30 years this chair has traveled back and forth across the country with me, and, with the exception of the seat and back cloth material, it is as solid today as it was the day I found it.

If you like lathe work, THIS PROJECT IS FOR YOU. This simple chair has 15 individually different turnings and a total of 31 turnings. All 31 turnings are simple and should not be difficult to make.

At one time, most platform rockers were made of mahogany, walnut or oak, but for this project, and for today's living, maple, cherry or any hardwood could be used for a very beautiful chair. To save a little material and the time of turning square pieces into diameters, large round dowels could be used as they can be readily purchasd in diameters of 2" or more.

Platform Rocker

by John A. Nelson

PHOTOGRAPH BY DEBORAH PORTER

INSTRUCTIONS

As with any project, carefully study the two-view drawing of the chair illustrating the front view and the right side view. Note the various turnings, part numbers, A through O and the three different 1¾" thick flat parts, parts P, Q and R. Be sure you fully understand how all parts are assembled before starting anything.

Make each of the turnings per each of the dimensioned illustrations. Take care to make tight fitting end diameters where the turnings are glued into mating holes. You may want to drill a hole into a piece of scrap wood using the same drill you will be using for the holes on the chair. Then make a ''test'' turning to determine the exact size turning you will need for a good tight fit.

Short turnings, such as the 1½″ diameter part G and the two part J's, could be turned as one unit and parted into individual parts when completed. The four identical part I's could also be turned as one unit and parted when completed. Part H can be simply cut from a ½″ diameter dowel. Take care in drilling part A. There must be a mating pair of parts—that is a right hand and left hand pair.

Draw the shape of parts P, Q and R on a sheet of heavy paper using a full size ½″ square grid and copying the shapes per the given illustrations. Transfer these shapes to the pieces of wood and cut out the parts. Carefully locate and drill all holes in the parts, but be sure to make a matching pair of all three parts (one right hand and one left hand). Sand all surfaces until smooth. The arc of the part P must be a perfect 14½″ radius with no irregular waves. The chair will not rock smoothly unless this arc is very smooth. Do not "round" the edges too much as they should be somewhat sharp. Using a router and a V-groove bit, cut the simple designs approximately 1/8″ deep, as illustrated, into the outer surfaces of parts P and Q. Using an 1/8″ radius bit, cut the edge of part R, 12 5/8″ long as illustrated.

ASSEMBLY

After all parts have been carefully made, the chair is actually very easy to put together. Think of the chair simply as four subassemblies—the back subassembly, the arm subassembly, the rocker subassembly and the base subassembly.

Glue the back subassembly together on a flat surface using parts A,B,C,D,E,F,G,H, and O. Keep all joints square and the subassembly flat.

Glue the two arm subassemblies together on a flat surface using parts J,K,L and M. Keep all parts flat.

Glue the rocker subassembly together using parts I,N,P and R. Keep this subassembly square, also. Drill for and set the 8 finish nails from underneath through part P and into part I, through part R and into part I.

Glue the base subassembly together using parts Q and N as shown, keeping everything square. Be sure all the feet

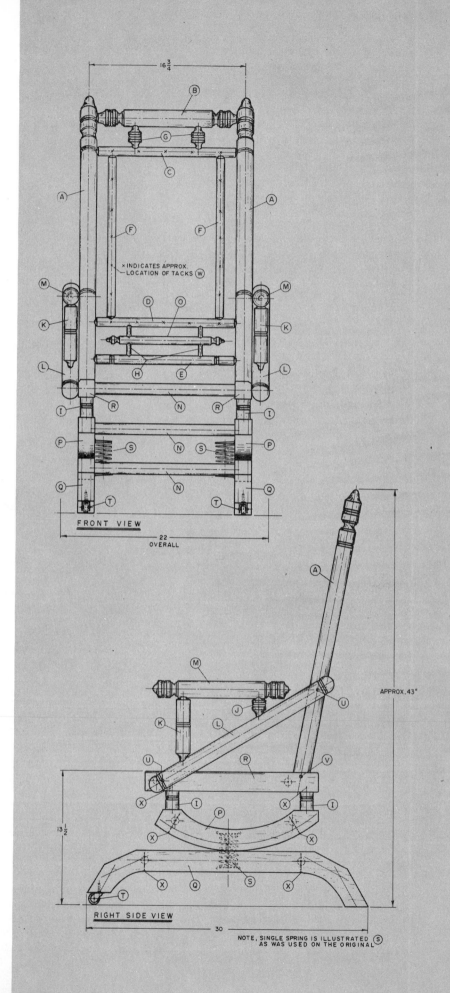

44

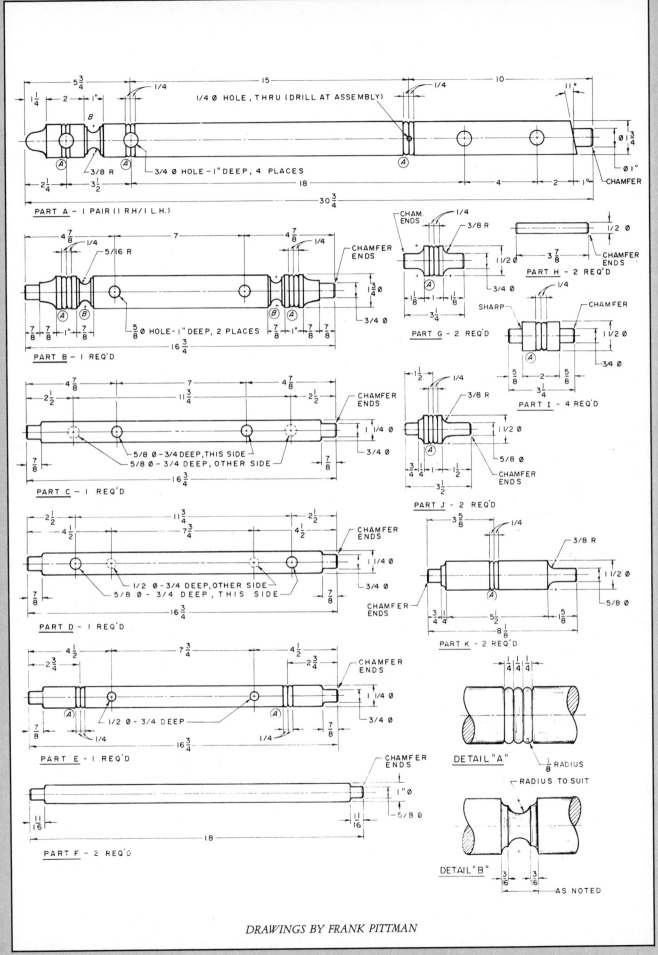

PART A – I PAIR (I R.H./I L.H.)

1/4 Ø HOLE, THRU (DRILL AT ASSEMBLY)

3/8 R

3/4 Ø HOLE – I" DEEP, 4 PLACES

CHAMFER

PART B – I REQ'D

5/16 R

CHAMFER ENDS

5/8 Ø HOLE – I" DEEP, 2 PLACES

PART C – I REQ'D

CHAMFER ENDS

5/8 Ø – 3/4 DEEP, THIS SIDE
5/8 Ø – 3/4 DEEP, OTHER SIDE

PART D – I REQ'D

CHAMFER ENDS

1/2 Ø – 3/4 DEEP, OTHER SIDE
5/8 Ø – 3/4 DEEP, THIS SIDE

PART E – I REQ'D

CHAMFER ENDS

1/2 Ø – 3/4 DEEP

PART F – 2 REQ'D

CHAMFER ENDS

PART G – 2 REQ'D

CHAM. ENDS

3/8 R

3/4 Ø

PART H – 2 REQ'D

CHAMFER ENDS

SHARP

CHAMFER

PART I – 4 REQ'D

3/8 R

PART J – 2 REQ'D

CHAMFER ENDS

3/8 R

PART K – 2 REQ'D

CHAMFER ENDS

DETAIL "A"

1/8 RADIUS

RADIUS TO SUIT

DETAIL "B"

AS NOTED

DRAWINGS BY FRANK PITTMAN

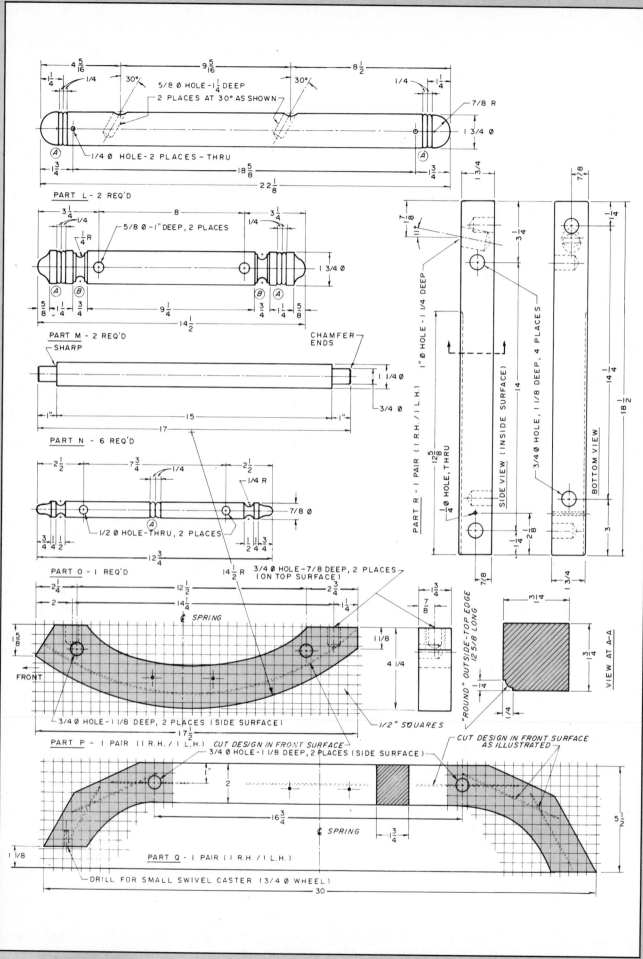

4 5/16   9 5/16   8 1/2
1/4   1/4   30°   5/8 Ø HOLE-1 1/4 DEEP   30°   1/4   1 1/4   7/8 R
2 PLACES AT 30° AS SHOWN   1 3/4 Ø
Ⓐ   1/4 Ø HOLE-2 PLACES-THRU   Ⓐ
1 3/4   18 5/8   1 3/4
22 1/8

PART L - 2 REQ'D

3 1/4   8   3 1/4
1/4   5/8 Ø-1" DEEP, 2 PLACES   1/4
1/4 R   1 3/4 Ø
Ⓐ Ⓑ   Ⓑ Ⓐ
5/8 1 1/4 3/4   9 1/4   3/4 1 1/4 5/8
14 1/2

PART M - 2 REQ'D

SHARP   CHAMFER ENDS
1 1/4 Ø
1"   15   1"   3/4 Ø
17

PART N - 6 REQ'D

2 1/2   7 3/4   1/4   2 1/2
1/4 R
7/8 Ø
Ⓐ
3/4 1 1/4 1/2   1/2 1/4 3/4
1/2 Ø HOLE-THRU, 2 PLACES
12 3/4

PART O - 1 REQ'D

3/4 Ø HOLE-7/8 DEEP, 2 PLACES
(ON TOP SURFACE)
14 1/2 R
2 1/4   12 1/2   2 3/4
2   14 1/4   1 1/4   3/4
Ⓛ SPRING   7/8
1 5/8   1 1/8
FRONT   4 1/4
3/4 Ø HOLE-1 1/8 DEEP, 2 PLACES (SIDE SURFACE)   1/2" SQUARES
17 1/2

PART P - 1 PAIR (I.R.H. / I.L.H.)   CUT DESIGN IN FRONT SURFACE
3/4 Ø HOLE-1 1/8 DEEP, 2 PLACES (SIDE SURFACE)   CUT DESIGN IN FRONT SURFACE AS ILLUSTRATED
1"
2
16 3/4   3/4   Ⓛ SPRING
1 1/8   5 1/2

PART Q - 1 PAIR (I.R.H. / I.L.H.)
DRILL FOR SMALL SWIVEL CASTER (3/4 Ø WHEEL)
30

1 3/4   7/8
7/8 11/8   3 1/4   1/4
1" Ø HOLE - 1/4 DEEP
14   14 1/4   18 1/2
3/4 Ø HOLE, 1 1/8 DEEP, 4 PLACES
12 5/8
1 Ø HOLE, THRU
1/4 Ø HOLE - 1 1/4 DEEP
2 1/8
1/4   3
7/8   1 3/4
SIDE VIEW (INSIDE SURFACE)   BOTTOM VIEW

PART R - 1 PAIR (I.R.H. / I.L.H.)

3 1/4
3 1/4
1/4   1/4
VIEW AT A-A
"ROUND" OUTSIDE-TOP EDGE 12 5/8 LONG

set square so the base will not rock. Drill for and set the 4 finish nails from underneath through part Q and into part N. This completes the four subassemblies.

Assemble the back subassembly to the rocker subassembly using glue and the two round head screws, part V. Attach the LOWER part of the arm subassemblies to the rocker and back subassemblies using two 4″ long, ¼″ diameter carriage bolts, washer and square nut, part U.

Locate the arm subassemblies into position and using the UPPER hole in part L as a template, drill a ¼″ diameter hole through both part A's as shown. Attach the two arm subassemblies using the other two, 4″ long, ¼″ diameter carriage bolts, part U. Refer to the right side view illustration.

Add the two swivel wheels to the front feet of part Q. Attach all three above subassemblies to the base subassembly with the two springs, part S. Center the springs on the center lines as shown on the illustrations of parts P and Q. Adjust tension on the springs by spacing the upper and lower parts of the spring, either closer together or farther apart. The seat should lean backwards slightly more than as shown on the drawing. Test the seat and adjust the springs to suit.

FINISHING

If oak or any open-pored hardwood is used, it should be filled before staining and finishing. Stain using a stain of your choice and finish using any good finishing process. Follow recommended instructions on the containers.

ADDING CLOTH HEADREST, BACK AND SEAT

HEADREST

Using two pieces of material, (I used heavy, velour type corduroy) measure the material 10½″ wide × 9″ long. This measurement allows for a ½″ seam all the way around. Measure a piece of batting material 10″ wide × 8½″ long. This will fit between the two pieces of material. Sew the two pieces of material together inside out, allowing ½″ seams, leaving one end opened. When the three sides are sewn together, fit the batting material in and turn the material right side out with the batting material in it. Turn the last seam in and handstitch it together. Put this on the headrest of the rocker and pin it together at the seams; handstitch together. One end will overlap the other where you have to pin it and handstitch it together.

BACK

Using two pieces of material 21″ long × 15″ wide, make the piece for the back of the chair. This measurement will allow ½″ seams all the way around the material for sewing it together. Follow the instructions above given for the headrest to put this piece together. Remember to measure the batting material ½″ smaller all the way around, 20½″ × 14½″. When you are finished sewing this together, tack the back to the back of the chair with upholstery tacks all the way around.

SEAT

Using two pieces of material 26″ long × 17″ wide make the piece for the seat of the chair. This measurement allows a ½″ seam all the way around the material for sewing it together. The batting material is measured ½″ smaller all the way around, 25½″ long × 16½″ wide. Put the seat together and sew as above for back and headrest. When

PARTS LIST		
PART	OVERALL SIZE	REQ'D
A	1 3/4 DIA - 30 3/4 LONG	2 •
B	1 3/4 DIA - 16 3/4 LONG	1
C	1 1/4 DIA - 16 3/4 LONG	1
D	1 1/4 DIA - 16 3/4 LONG	1
E	1 1/4 DIA - 16 3/4 LONG	1
F	1 DIA — 18 LONG	2
G	1 1/2 DIA - 3 1/4 LONG	2
H	1/2 DIA - 3 7/8 LONG	2
I	1 1/2 DIA - 3 1/4 LONG	4
J	1 1/2 DIA - 3 1/2 LONG	2
K	1 1/2 DIA - 8 1/8 LONG	2
L	1 3/4 DIA - 22 1/8 LONG	2
M	1 3/4 DIA - 14 1/2 LONG	2
N	1 1/4 DIA - 17 LONG	6
O	7/8 DIA - 12 3/4 LONG	1
P	1 3/4 X 4 1/4 - 17 1/2 LONG	2 •
Q	1 3/4 X 5 1/2 - 30 LONG	2 •
R	1 3/4 X 1 3/4 - 18 1/2 LONG	2 •
S	SPRING ASSEMBLY	2
T	SWIVEL CASTER (3/4 DIA)	2
U	CARRIAGE BOLT W/WASHER AND SQUARE NUT	4
V	SCREW-ROUND HEAD	2
W	BRASS TACKS 1/2″ LONG	AS REQ'D
X	FINISH NAIL 10d	12

• MAKE ONE R.H. AND ONE L.H.

finished sewing it together, tack it underneath to the back and front round turnings of the chair. Before you put the material on the seat portion, you should make up a support for the seat. I used a canvas type material, one piece 38″ long and 17″ wide with two to three layers of batting in between the canvas type material for a support. Remember, measure your batting material smaller than the canvas material. Take the canvas, with the batting material in between and sew this together. Then wrap all this around the back and front wood turnings, folding under a 1″ seam allowance where both ends meet. Staple or tack to the two round turnings at the back and front of the chair.

This is the way I did my pieces for the headrest, back, and seat. It is only a suggestion as how to make them. Perhaps you can come up with a better way.

Sit back and enjoy—this rocker will be around for many, many years to come.

SUPPLIERS

Spring H-5520, Cotton batting H-9654 Upholstery nails H-9680 and turning squares can be purchased from CRAFTSMAN WOOD SERVICE, 1735 West Cortland Ct., Adderson, IL 60101.

Swivel casters C-1 (¾″ diameter wheel) can be purchased from ANGLO-AMERICAN BRASS CO., 4146 Mitzi Rd., Box 9792, San Jose, CA 95157-0792.

ABOUT THE AUTHOR:

John A. Nelson is a contributing editor to The American Woodworker.

Fireplace Bench

By Franklin H. Gottshall

The Fireplace Bench, shown in the photograph, is a piece of furniture I designed and made while a student in college fifty-five years ago. The wood I used to make it is red gum, but other woods, like walnut, birch, or maple could be substituted to build another like it.

The bench may be put to other uses in addition to the original purpose for which it was intended. In our house it more often serves as a table in front of the sofa, to hold magazines, or from which to serve snacks and drinks to guests, than as a bench upon which to be seated.

Being an amateur designer of furniture at this early stage of my career, there are certain features I would change to make it a better piece of furniture if I were to build another like it today. With this in mind, the structural alterations I have made on my drawings, from those found on the bench shown in the photograph, change its appearance only slightly, but strengthen its frame structurally.

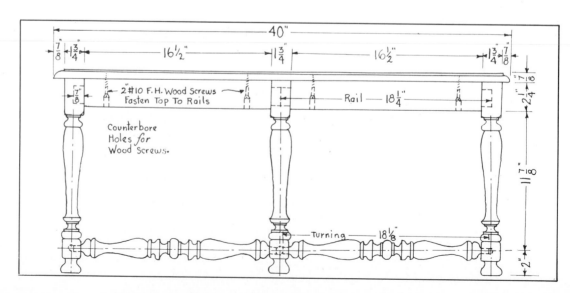

FIGURE 6.

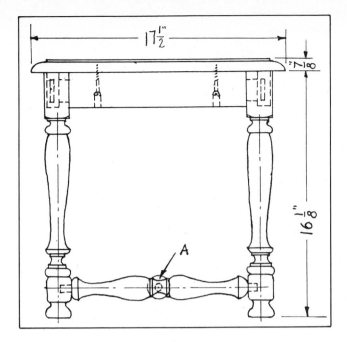

FIGURE 2.

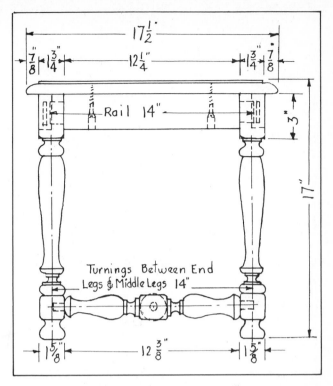

FIGURE 7.

Figure 2 shows the end of the bench as it appears in the photograph. At 'A', in Figure 2, the long stretcher (Figure 3) is joined to a very thin area of the turned short stretcher. Holes drilled into the three turned short stretchers to make these joints, further weaken this area on the short stretchers, so I have redesigned these short stretchers, as shown in Figure 4, thereby greatly strengthening these joints. This improved construction is shown in Figure 7.

To make another improvement in the original design, I've substituted flush joints for the offset joints found where rails supporting the top are joined to the legs. Figure 8 shows how these two kinds of joints differ from each other. This structural change makes it possible to lengthen tenons on the rails, and deepen mortises on the legs, which results in stronger glue joints. Flush joints were more widely used on older hand-built furniture and, in my estimation, improve the appearance on the type of furniture shown here.

In the side and end views of the assembled bench, note the change I've made in the shape of the molding around the edges of the bench top. In Figure 2, and on the left end of the top, shown in Figure 6, the quarter-round part of the molding ends with a sharp edge at the bottom, a feature not well suited to a seat. The rounded thumbnail shape of this molding, shown in Figure 7, and at the right end of Figure 6, is more suitable, both from the standpoint of appearance and comfort.

Figure 5 gives dimensions to turn the six legs. Mortise-and-tenon joints are used to join legs to the rails to which the top is fastened with 2'' #10 wood screws, as shown in Figures 2, 6 and 7. Construction details showing how rail and leg joints are made is shown in Figure 9.

Oil stain, made from burnt umber color in oil, thinned with turpentine to a consistency transparent enough so as not to hide the wood grain, was used to color the bench. Soft cotton rags should be used to wipe off all excess stain as soon as it has been applied, and then left to dry for at least 48 hours in a warm, dry room. A high grade of glossy floor varnish was

used for the next two coats, since red gum does not require a coat of wood filler, it not being a porous-grained wood. The first coat of varnish, which acts as a sealer over the stain, was thinned with an equal amount of turpentine, and applied with a bristle brush, and allowed to dry thoroughly. Surfaces were then smoothed down with 00 steel wool. The top was also gone over with fine-grit garnet paper, after which all dust was carefully removed from all surfaces.

A second coat of glossy varnish, this time undiluted, was then put on, and allowed to dry in a warm dry room. If the bench is to be rubbed down with powdered pumice stone and oil to give it a satin-like finish, a third coat of glossy varnish is recommended. Paint manufacturers have developed a very durable type of varnish which dries to a satin finish without rubbing as it dries and hardens, which is a good, and almost equally beautiful final coat for furniture, eliminating, as it does the harder task of rubbing and polishing with the pumice and rubbing oil.

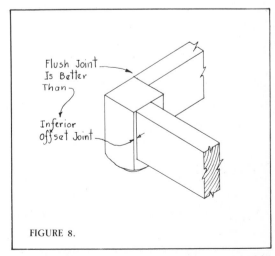

FIGURE 8.

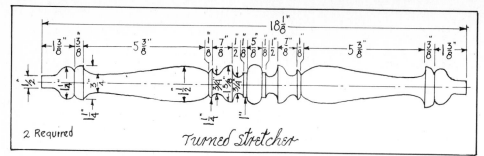

2 Required   *Turned Stretcher*

FIGURE 3.

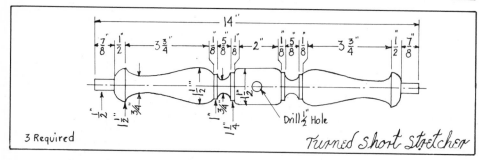

3 Required   *Turned Short Stretcher*

FIGURE 4.

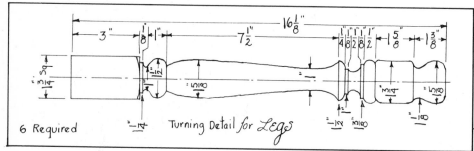

6 Required   *Turning Detail for Legs*

FIGURE 5.

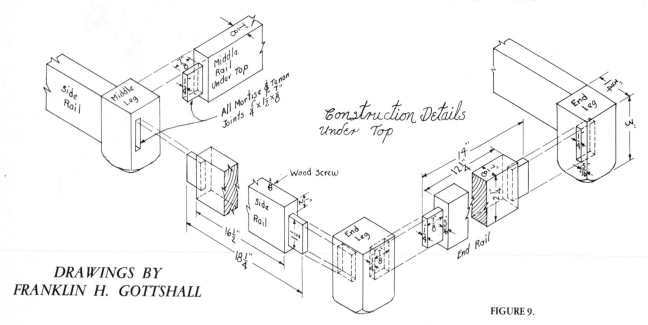

Construction Details Under Top

All Mortise & Tenon Joints 1/4" x 1/2" x 7/8"

Wood screw

DRAWINGS BY
FRANKLIN H. GOTTSHALL

FIGURE 9.

BILL OF MATERIAL

1 Top . . . . 7/8" x 17½" x 40"	6 Legs. . . . . 1¾" x 1¾" x 16 1/8"
4 Side Rails . . . . 7/8" x 2¼" x 18¼"	3 Short Rails (2 end, 1 middle) . . 7/8" x 2¼" x 14"
2 Turned Stretchers . . 15/8" diam. x 181/8"	3 Turned Short Stretchers . . 1½" diam. x 14"

50

Child's Cradle
An Heirloom For Generations To Come

by R. B. Rennaker

A child's cradle is a piece of household furniture that could easily become a family heirloom. Except for the spindles, it is not difficult to make. You may choose to turn them on your own lathe, as I did, or you might want to purchase them. They are available at most woodworking outlets. I chose black walnut as the material, but the cradle would look good using any number of species. I made all pieces so they could be easily disassembled, using wood inserts and stove bolts. If you do not see the possibility of having to take the cradle apart some day, you may wish to use wood screws and glue. The plans for this cradle are a "second

generation" design and differ slightly from the photograph.

If you are going to turn your own spindles, they should be constructed first. Twenty-two spindles are required for the two sides at 11½" long and ten for the ends at 14½" long. Note that ½" is inserted into the rails on each end, leaving 10½" and 13½" respectively, between the top and bottom rails. You may use any pattern you wish in turning down the spindles. I used a very simple pattern. I first cut the stock ¾" square and one inch longer than required, turning each down to ½" diameter before turning the pattern. This will make for a more uniform pattern when

CHILD'S CRADLE

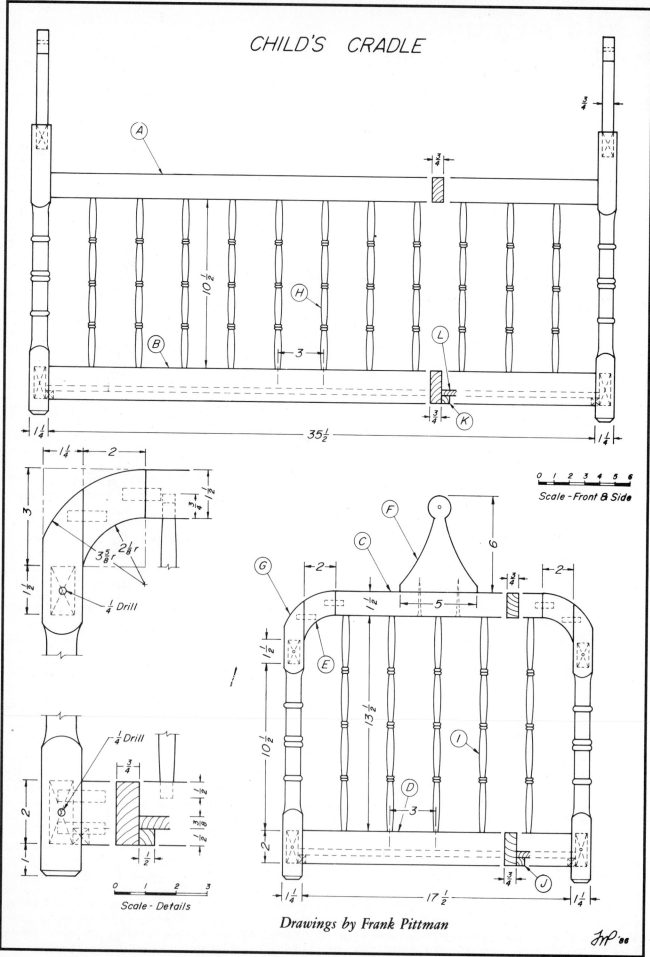

Scale - Front & Side

Scale - Details

Drawings by Frank Pittman

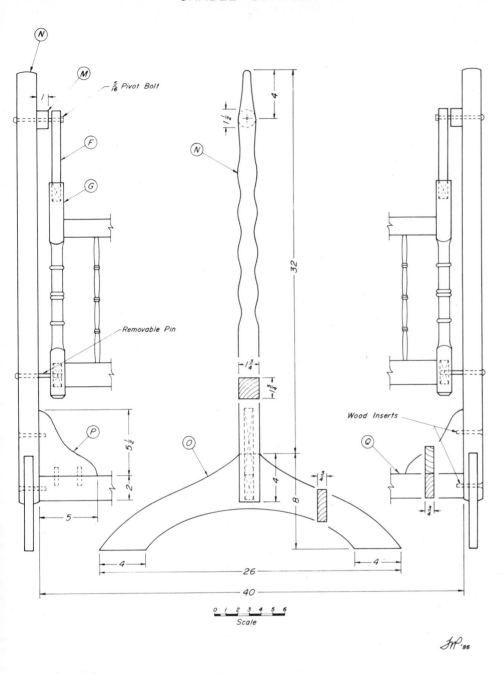

gluing the spindles to the rails. Use one at each end and one in the center. They will insure that the inside distance between the top and bottom rails is exactly 10½". An extra ¼" has been allowed at the top for proper alignment in case some spindles are slightly longer than others. Clamp securely using pipe clamps. Use your square to be sure the assembly comes out true. If it is not, use a diagonal clamp to pull in to square.

ENDS

The bottom rail for the end is exactly like the bottom rail on the sides except that it is only 17½" long. Instead of wood inserts, drill two 3/8" holes ¾" deep in each end for dowels. The top rails are 1½" X 13½" long with a single dowel hole in each end. Cut two pieces 2" X 3" X 1¼" thick (Part E). Be sure the wood grain runs lengthwise, ie., the 3" dimension. Drill a dowel hole ¾" from the top on one side and ¾" from the bottom on the opposite side. Be sure these holes are centered in the 1¼" thick edge. Dowel and glue these pieces to each end of both top rails. Drill two holes through the top rails to take #10 flathead wood screws 2½" long. Countersink from the bottom side.

The next step is to construct the end posts. Finished, they must be 1¼" square and 18" long. Be sure you leave them square at both ends where the rails join. We are ready now to assemble the end sections. Mark the center of both rails and every 3" each side of the center. Drill 3/8" holes ½" deep in the bottom and ¾" deep in the top. Drill two dowel holes in each end of the bottom rail.

Cut two pieces of scrap exactly 13½" long for spaces just as we did on the side assemblies. Glue and drive the spindles into the bottom rail, then glue and drive the top rail down on to the spindles with the scrap spacers at each end. Clamp until set, but be sure they are square before the glue sets. Using dowel pin markers, mark the two dowel holes in the bottom of the corner post. Leave 1" below the bottom rail. Mark the single dowel hole in the top of the end post (which has not yet been cut off). Drill the dowel holes in the end posts. Apply glue to the dowels and clamp the end posts to the

finished. I marked the locations on the tool rest and turned each to size using a caliper. Each end must be tapered to a 3/8" diameter to insert in 3/8" holes in the bottom and top rails.

The holes for the spindles are 3" apart on centers. Find the center of the rail and mark for the center spindle, then, every 3" out to the end. Due to the end posts, the last space will not be exactly 3". This is the reason for starting in the center. Be sure the holes are in the center of the ¾" rail. Use a self centering device to mark or drill the holes. Drill ½" deep in the bottom rail and ¾" deep in the top rail. I shall explain why later. I used ¼" X 20 wood inserts at all removable joints. This requires a 7/16" hole in each end of each rail. Drill ¾" deep and be sure the holes are in the exact center of the ends. Screw the wood inserts in flush with the end of the rails.

Along the lower inside edge of each side rail, nail and glue a ½" X ½" strip (Part K) flush with the bottom edge. These strips will retain the bottom of the cradle when finished. Note that the bottom rail is 2" wide while the top rail is 1½" wide. Both are ¾" thick. Using glue, assemble the spindles in the bottom rail first, driving to the depth of the hole. Now drive the top rail down on to the spindles. Cut three pieces of scrap 10½" long. Place these pieces between the top and bottom rail when center assembly. When the glue has set, saw off the top corner in a rounded fashion. This is the finished end section.

You will need two pieces 5″ wide and 6″ long to make the cradle hangers (Part F). Cut to desired shape leaving a 1½″ partial circle at the top. Glue and screw to the top of the rail as shown. When the end sections are completed, saw off the top corners as indicated in the detail drawing. I left these corners square to make it easy to clamp during the gluing process.

The end support posts are 1¾″ square and 36″ in length. Extend the two outside pieces 4″ below the center piece to accept the leg pieces later. Cut to the desired pattern leaving the same amount of material on each side of the center piece. You may turn or saw any pattern you wish on these posts, but be sure and leave about 12″ at the bottom.

The "foot" sections are made as shown, 26″ long and 8″ from top to bottom of the foot. Four inches is about right for the feet. A "knob" (Part M) 1½″ in diameter is turned to round and glued to the end post 4″ from the top. When the glue is set, drill a 5/16″ hole through both the end post and the knob.

The cross brace (Part Q) and the brackets (Part P) are made next. When finished, the cross brace must be 40″ long, but leave it a little longer so that the ends can be squared later. The brackets are 5″ X 5½″ with two dowel holes in the 5″ edge and one in the 5½″ edge. Glue and dowel to Part Q flush with the end. When the glue has set, cut to the shape shown. Trim the ends square until the total length is 40″. It is most important that these ends be square as they are the only support for the support posts, and they should be exactly vertical.

Assemble the feet into the end posts and glue and clamp, being sure the post is exactly at right angles to the feet. Use wood inserts again to attach the posts to the cross brace. Drill ¼″ holes where marked on Part N and counterbore a

½″ hole 3/8″ deep on the outside. This is to accept the wood "buttons" to hide the screw holes. This must be done at all holes for the insert bolts. If you use wood screws and glue, you will also need to use the wood buttons to hide the screw heads.

Before the cradle is assembled drill a 5/16″ pivot screw hole through the top of Part N as shown. On a flat surface lay the end assembly and one side assembly together so that the bottom rails match. Then mark for the holes in the corner posts. Do this for all four corners. Drill ¼″ holes through all end posts as marked, then countersink 3/8″ by ½″ deep to accept the trim "buttons".

Assemble the sides and ends with ¼″ stove bolts 1½″ long. Measure for the bottom and use any kind of material for this. The corners will have to be "snipped" a tiny bit so that it will fit around the end posts and lay flat along the ½″ strip nailed to the bottom rail.

Use 5/16″ machine bolts 4″ long to hang the cradle between the support posts. If you use wood inserts in the end posts, you will want to countersink for the trim buttons as we did on the cradle corner posts. Draw up these bolts just tight enough so the cradle will swing easily.

If a locked position is required for the cradle, 3/8″ holes may be drilled through the end post and into the center of the end section bottom rail. A length of 3/8″ dowel stock may be inserted through both holes for locking the cradle in a stationary position.

If your cradle is assembled with wood screws and glue, then the wood trim buttons may also be glued in place. If you have used the wood inserts and you think you may someday want to disassemble your cradle, then the buttons should not be glued in place.

I fashioned a "bearing" for the hole in the hangar (Part F) out of a scrap piece of metal tubing of the correct size to accept the 5/16″ machine bolts. This is not actually necessary as the cradle swings well without any such bearing.

After a thorough sanding with 220 grit sandpaper, the cradle can be finished with your favorite finish. I used two coats of satin polyurethane.

"I chose black walnut as the material, but the cradle would look good using any number of species."

Bill of Materials

CODE	DESCRIPTION	T	W	L	PCS
A	Top Side Rails	¾″	1½″	35½″	2
B	Bottom Side Rails	¾″	2″	35½″	2
C	Top End Rails	¾″	1½″	13½″	2
D	Bottom End Rails	¾″	2″	17½″	2
E	Corner Pieces	1¼″	2″	3″	4
F	Cradle Hangers	¾″	5″	6″	2
G	End Posts	1¼″	1¼″	18″	4
H	Side Spindles	½″ dia. x 11½″			22
I	End Spindles	½″ dia. x 14½″			10
J	Bottom Strips	½″	½″	18″	2
K	Bottom Strips	½″	½″	36″	2
L	Bottom	3/8″	18″	36″	1
M	Knob	1″	1½″	1½″	2
N	Cradle Support Post	1¾″	1¾″	36″	2
O	Foot	¾″	8″	26″	2
P	Brackets	¾″	5½″	5″	2
Q	Support Rail	¾″	2″	40″	1

HARDWARE:

¼-20 Wood Inserts 12

¼-20 Flathead Stove Bolts . . 12

#10 X 2½″ Flat Head Wood
   Screws 4

5/16″ X 4″ Machine Bolts . . . 2

Buttons ½″ X 3/8″ 14

Dowel Pins 3/8″ X 1½″ 12

About the Author:

R.B. Rennaker is a woodworker living in Kokomo, Indiana.

CANNON BALL BEDSTEAD

by Carlyle Lynch

Photographs by Roy Early, Illustrations by Jennifer Chiles

Visitors to Fort Harrison, a Dayton, Virginia house museum, admire the crisp turnings on the maple posts of this eighteenth century bedstead thought to be from the area of Philadelphia, Pennsylvania. The balls are so perfect that a template would have to be used to reproduce them. Perhaps the thought has occurred to you, as it has to me, that the cannon ball on bedposts was an expression of patriotism like that of the American bald eagle carved and gilded on the top of mirror frames.

The posts were turned in one piece on a long bed lathe more commonly found in furniture shops two hundred years ago than now. The turning shows evidence of a man thoroughly familiar with deep cove cuts. Those of us less skilled can approximate that work by taking light cuts with really sharp, round nose turning chisels, and patient sanding. The post design is such that we can turn them on our 36″ long lathes in three sections, as suggested by broken lines showing large dowels turned on the top and middle (octagonal) sections to fit holes drilled in the sections beneath them. (See drill press set up for drilling central holes in columns.) Remember to cut sections at least 2″ longer to make the 1″ to 1½″ diam. dowels. Turn the dowels a bit oversize and leave centers on for fitting snug to the holes when those have been drilled. This will mean turning a plug from scrap for the hole in the top of the octagonal section. Make the posts in sections; cut the pieces for each from the same length of 4″ stock and match mark them to preserve the grain pattern. Remember that flats of the octagons must line up with the square sides of the bottom sections. Before gluing sections together, carve three tiny lateral v-grooves in the dowels (120° apart) to allow trapped air to escape. Have clamps ready.

Cut rail and headboard mortises after posts have been turned. All of these joints are dry, the parts held securely by eight bed bolts engaging nuts inserted in the rails and held there by wood plugs whose grain runs with that of the rails. Side rails of the original are slightly above the end rails, perhaps an oddity of the long ago builder that we need not follow. Two more things about the rails: First make short tenons—5/8″ is shown but ½″ is not too short. Long ones tend to snap off when setting up or taking down bolted beds. Make the mortises 1/8″ deeper than tenons are long to be sure bolts can pull rail shoulders tight to posts. Second, the rails of corded beds must be heavy (wide and thick) to withstand the inward pull of the cords when the bed is occupied. Notice also that the tenons on the headboard are full thickness of that member.

The bolts on this bed have large flat slotted heads without washers so that a large screw driver, rather than a special wrench, can be used. The heads fit into shallow sockets to be flush with post surfaces. One must therefore bore the shallow hole for the bolt head before boring for the bolt, and this is true for any style bolt whose head you want flush or below the surface.

CANNON BALL BEDSTEAD

Maple

Fort Harrison Museum Collection
Dayton, Virginia

About 1800

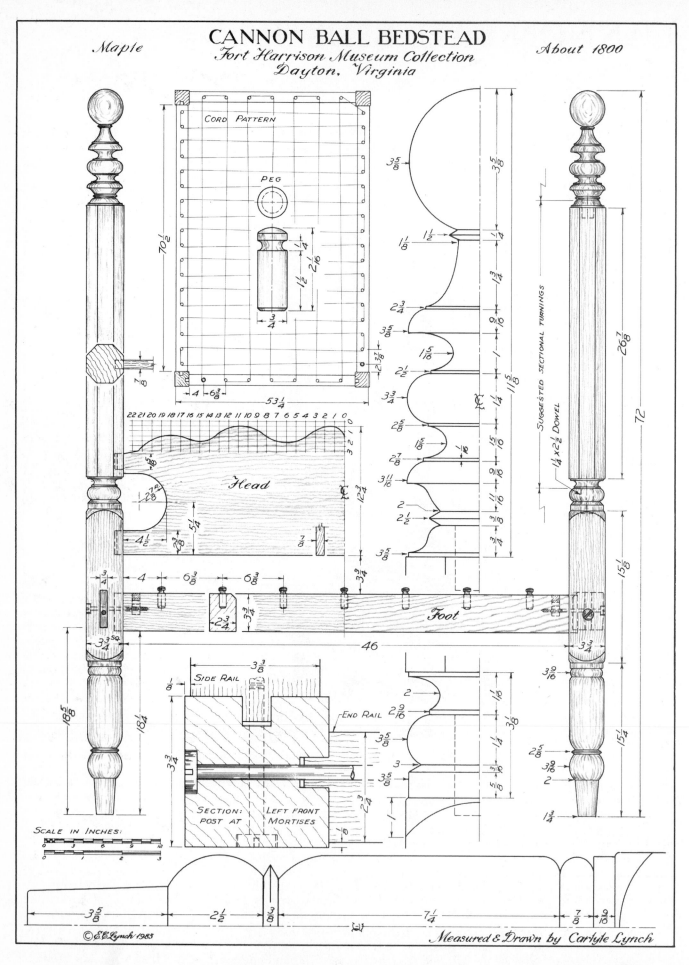

CORD PATTERN

PEG

Suggested sectional turnings

Head

Foot

SIDE RAIL

END RAIL

SECTION: LEFT FRONT
post at MORTISES

SCALE IN INCHES:

Measured & Drawn by Carlyle Lynch

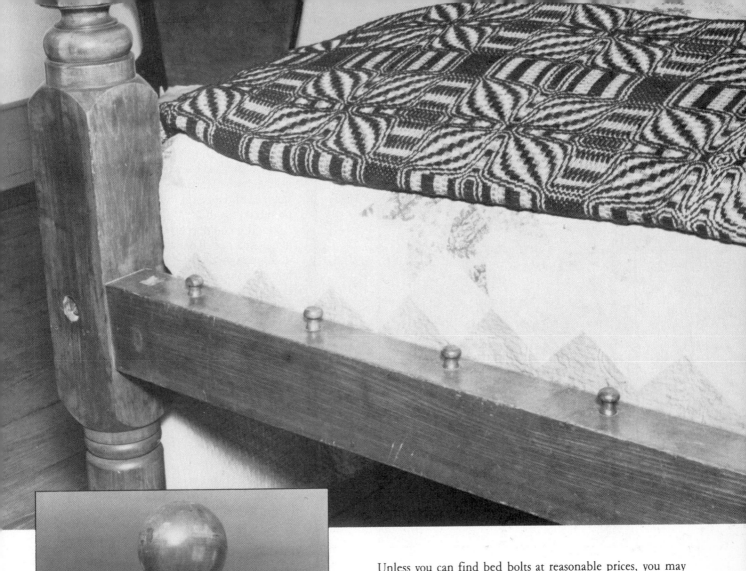

After boring the posts so the bolts will cross over each other, insert each marked rail tenon into its mortise and use a pointed bolt to spot where to drill the rail. Set up to drill the posts on a drill press. Then the holes through the posts can act as guides for drilling the rails. Bedstead builders often use a cold chisel to stamp posts and mating rail ends with Roman numerals to aid identifying parts.

Unless you can find bed bolts at reasonable prices, you may choose to make them, using regular 3/8″ x 6″ or 7″ hex-head bolts and flat washers. These should be turned, filed, or ground to about a 60° point to aid finding the hole in the nuts. Better nuts than regular hex nuts are ones made from short piece of mild steel flat bar to obtain a rectangular nut. For a 3/8″ bolt, the nut should be made from a piece of steel 3/8 x 5/8 x 3/4. Drill a 5/16″ diam. hole and use a 3/8-16 tap available from hardware stores. Of course, the nut sockets are cut in the rails after the bolt holes are made. Sockets out of sight are made from inside or from the bottoms of rails. The bed has some from the top and others from the front sides, but each is covered by a neatly made plug.

To be correct, bedding should be as wide as the rails, so that covers hang straight down. The size of this bed as shown is almost our standard, double bed size of 54″ wide x 75″ long rails. If you choose to cord the bed, with a slight increase in width and length, (see materials list), a standard innerspring mattress will rest on the side rails and allow the covers to hang straight. Cord pegs (which are driven in dry holes) have rounded tops and stick up just enough to hold the cord and so do not interfere with a mattress resting on them. If you have room for a queen size bed, increase rail sizes to allow a 54″ box spring to rest on angle irons and come flush with rail tops. Get a custom made mattress cut out around the front posts to rest on the front rail. The bed would then be 61¼″ x 79 5/8″. Angle irons should be set flush into rails about 14″ from posts and secured with 1″ x 12″ flat head screws.

The rich color of the maple appears to come from aging rather than stain. Naturally finished woods darken noticeably in a few years, so my choice for finish is one of the antique oil finishes which are penetrating, protective, clear, and very easy to apply.

STANDARD BED SIZES

Single - 39" wide x 75" long rails
Double - 54" wide x 75" long rails
Queen - 60" wide x 80" long rails
King - 76" wide x 80" long rails

SUGGESTION

Use a standard 54" box spring and 62" wide custom innerspring mattress cut out around the foot posts.

MATTRESS MADE TO FIT AROUND FOOT POSTS

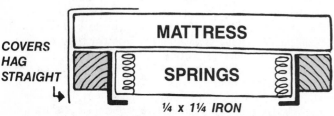

COVERS HAG STRAIGHT

MATTRESS

SPRINGS

¼ x 1¼ IRON

Material List:

All wood parts are hard maple. *(shoulder to shoulder = s-s)*

4 Posts	3¾ x 3¾ x 72½	½" allowance for lathe center
2 Side rails	3 3/8 x 3¾ x 71¾	70½ s-s (or 76¼, 75 s-s)
2 End rails	2¾ x 3¾ x 47¼	46 s-s (or 48, 46¾ s-s)
1 Headboard	7/8 x 12¾ x 47¼	46 s-s (or 48, 46¾ s-s)
50 Cord Pegs	¾ x ¾ x 2½	allowance for center

Supply Source

8 Bed bolts with nuts and special wrench, 3/8" x 6" or 7". Available from Ball and Ball, 463 W. Lincoln Hwy., Exton, Pa. 19341 or Horton Brasses, Box 95, Cromwell, CT. 06416.

150 feet Cotton sash cord, 5/16" diam., braided; available as window weight cord from hardware stores.

Superb quality bedding made to order can be had from Sunset Mattress Co., Box 35-L, Ossipee, NH 03864, 603-539-6256. This is an unsolicited recommendation.

ABOUT THE AUTHOR:

Carlyle Lynch is a retired teacher and cabinetmaker. He is a frequent contributor to The American Woodworker.

Drill through the center of a piece of 3/8" rod or dowel and thread four or five feet of fish line through it. Tie one end to a plumb bob. Chuck as shown and use to align plumb bob with pointed piece in drill table center hole. Clamp table in that position. Replace plumb bob with 1", 1¼" or 1½" spade bit. Support column to be drilled by placing its lathe center point on aligned point. Start drill and engage bit point with the top lathe center point and drill the column for the dowel.

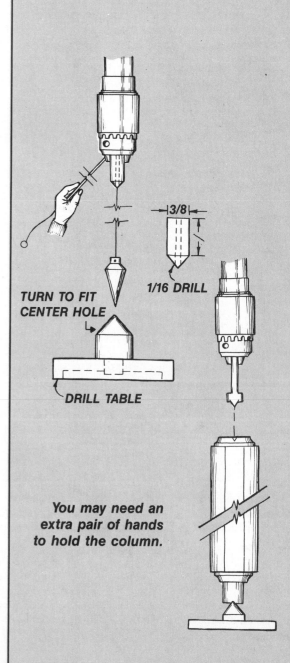

3/8

1/16 DRILL

TURN TO FIT CENTER HOLE

DRILL TABLE

You may need an extra pair of hands to hold the column.

Eli Terry Pillar And Scroll Clock

by Frank M. Pittman

Eli Terry was a well known American clock maker during the early part of the nineteenth century. The pillar and scroll clock, which first appeared in about 1814, was one of his most famous designs. The dimensions of the clock in this article are very close to those of his original clocks. The greatest change is in the depth of the case. Original clocks were only four inches deep. This depth is insufficient for some modern movements so it was increased to 4 15/16″. The door frame is also made slightly heavier than some originals. It is important to remember that if you change the door design you must consider the painted glass and clock face size.

If you are interested in reproducing a Terry clock exactly, you might refer to an article by Frederick J. Bryant, "Reproducing a Rare Old Clock", *Popular Science Monthly,* September 1929. A good library might have old issues of this magazine. The best way, of course, would be to measure an original, if you are lucky enough to locate one.

An important first step in clock making is to obtain the movement, face and related hardware. The Mason and Sullivan Company, 586 Higgins Crowel Road, West Yarmouth, Cape Cod, MA 02673, has all of the necessary supplies; in fact, they also sell Pillar and Scroll clock plans and a kit. I based this design around the Mason and Sullivan components. You could also obtain parts from other vendors.

Material Selection

Early clocks of this style were made from mahogany with many of the parts being veneered. If you are interested in making an accurate reproduction, mahogany should be your choice. Walnut and cherry are also used today with this design, and I have seen some beautiful, curly maple Terry clocks. The clock pictured in this article was made from walnut.

Case Construction

It is best to begin construction by making the basic case (parts #10, 12, 13, & 14). The two sides (#12 & 13) are made from 3/4″ solid walnut. After these pieces are cut to finished size, a rabbet 3/8″ x 13/16″ is cut on the front edge of each piece. A 1/4″ x 3/8″ rabbet is cut on each end. These rabbets can be cut in a variety of ways depending on your equipment. I actually used a shaper to form the long edge rabbets and a table saw to do the short ones. After rabbeting, the front edge of the sides should be rounded over. This rounding over can be done by hand or with a router or shaper.

The inner top and bottom (part #14) and the back fins (part #10) can be made from resawn 1/4″ walnut. It is easier to resaw all of these parts at the same time. I generally resaw the pieces to approximately 5/16″ thickness and then surface them to final thickness on a planer. The outside edge of the back fins should be rounded over with a router cut or by hand.

The basic case can now be assembled using #5 x 5/8″ flat head screws. The inner top and bottom are screwed to the sides and the back fins are screwed to the back of the sides. Assemble this unit first with screws only and check for squareness. Take the assembly apart and sand all of the parts before final assembly. After sanding is complete, apply glue to the rabbets and reassemble.

ELI TERRY
PILLAR & SCROLL CLOCK
Circa - 1814

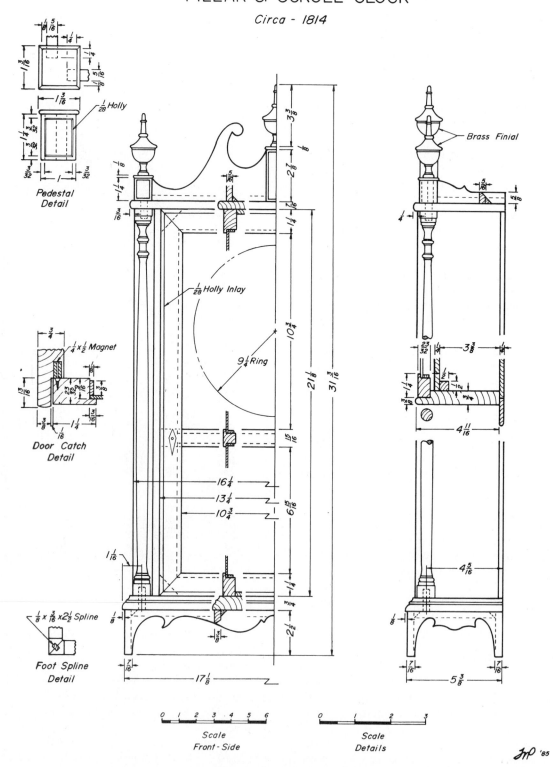

Pedestal
Detail

$\frac{1}{28}$ Holly

$\frac{1}{28}$ Holly Inlay

$10\frac{3}{4}$

$9\frac{1}{4}$ Ring

Door Catch
Detail

$\frac{1}{4} \times \frac{1}{2}$ Magnet

$\frac{1}{8} \times \frac{3}{16} \times 2\frac{1}{4}$ Spline

Foot Spline
Detail

Brass Finial

$16\frac{1}{4}$
$13\frac{1}{4}$
$10\frac{3}{4}$

$1\frac{1}{16}$

$17\frac{1}{8}$

$4\frac{11}{16}$

$4\frac{5}{16}$

$5\frac{3}{8}$

Scale
Front - Side

Scale
Details

JↄP '85

Drawing by Frank Pittman

Base and Feet

I have found that it is better when making the base (part #23) to cut the piece to finished length and about 1/8" over width to begin with. Then cut the molding on the ends and front edge. The extra width is ripped off after the molding is cut to remove any chip-out that may occur on the back edge. A router and router table can be used to cut this molding.

The feet are cut from 3/8" stock. To prepare the legs, first rip the stock to a finished width of 2 1/2". Leave the front piece about one inch over length. The stock for the side pieces should be long enough for both sides plus some waste, or about 12". It is much easier to handle the side pieces as one long length while mitering. Next, cut a miter on one end of the front foot blank, measure from this cut to finished length, and cut the second miter. Now, cut a miter on each end of the 12" side foot blank. Locate the spline cuts carefully on the miters so the groove will not cut into the leg pattern. Make the spline cuts across each miter using a table saw. The 12" side foot blank can now be cut into finished lengths of 5 7/16".

A full size one-half symmetrical pattern should be made of the front and side feet. This can be made from thin cardboard or index card stock. Using the pattern, lay out the front and side curves with a pencil. Saw out the curved shapes on a jig saw or band saw. Drum sand the curves to remove the saw marks and smooth out the curves.

Next, cut the two splines to fit the spline slots in the legs. Make these splines with the grain running opposite the grain on the legs. This will help strengthen the otherwise weak cross-grain leg.

When gluing the leg miters, first glue the spline in one side of the miter and let it dry for about 15 minutes. Then glue the other half of the miter in place. It seems a little easier to control everything this way. Rubber bands and spring clamps can be used to hold the miters closed while they dry.

Next, center the leg assembly on the base and glue it in place. The back feet (part #27) can be made and glued in place. This small part adds a great deal of strength to the rear legs. Reinforce the legs further by gluing small triangular corner blocks between the base and leg all the way around and behind each corner joint.

To give the clock a more delicate look, carve a small chamfer behind the legs and curved section as shown in the drawing. This same technique is also used on the broken pediment. You will find this detail on old clocks.

Crown and Broken Pediment

The crown base (part #7) is fabricated from 7/16" stock. It is best to leave this part about 1/8" over width until after the molding is cut to allow for possible chip-out. Parts #4 & 5, broken pediment, look much better if they are book matched. Try to find a small crotch or curly figured piece of walnut in your stock. If you select and prepare the pediment stock carefully, you will really add a touch of class to the overall design. After you have found the right material, resaw it and smooth to final thickness. Next, square the

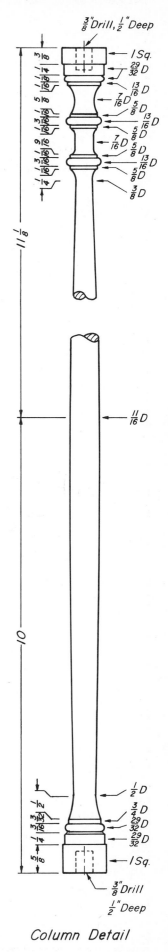

Column Detail

pediment pieces to length on a table saw. Using a cardboard template, transfer the curves to the two blanks. Saw out the curves on a jig saw or band saw. I usually tape the two blanks together with double-faced tape then saw and drum sand them both at the same time. The small top section of each half of the pediment is very fragile and should be reinforced in some way. I use a veneer spline for added strength. If the spline is not used, the part would need to be made heavier, and this detracts from the overall design.

The crown pedestals (part #1 and 2) are made from 1" x 1" stock. The grooves should be cut in these pieces before they are cut into short lengths. After the pedestals have been grooved and cut to length, they should be inlaid. Inlay was not used on early clocks, but it seems to add a nice touch to the design. It is, of course, optional. I use 1/28" holly veneer for the inlay and make the cuts in the pedestals with a Dremel tool.

The broken pediment and pedestals can now be glued together. Before assembly, be sure to sand the pediment pieces through 220 paper. During the gluing operation, be sure that the parts are aligned properly and that the bottom of the assembly is flat. After this assembly is dry, carve a small chamfer on the back corner of the pediment as was done with the feet.

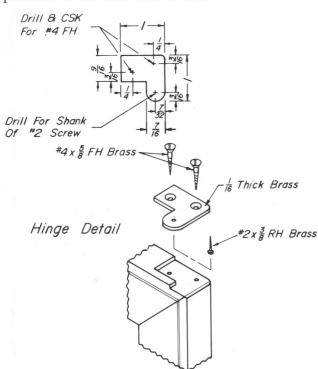

Hinge Detail

The 3/8" mounting holes for the columns should be located in the crown base and drilled. You can clamp these two parts together, matching center lines, and drill through both pieces at the same time. This hole location is very critical, so extra care must be taken to be sure that the columns will be positioned correctly.

Next, center the broken pediment over the crown base and glue it in place. Fabricate the side crown pieces (part #6) and glue them in place. To add strength, glue triangular corner blocks between the crown base, pediment, and side crowns.

The pedestals caps can now be fabricated from 1/8" walnut and glued to the top of the pedestals. These caps

should be installed so edge grain shows to the front, not end grain.

Columns

Turning the long slender columns is probably the most challenging task in the clock. They are challenging because of their length and delicacy. Begin the columns by cutting the 1" square pieces to finished length. They should be exactly the same length as the side pieces. I find it is easier to turn the long center section of the column first, then do the coves and beads at each end. This will minimize chatter. A steady rest can also be used to

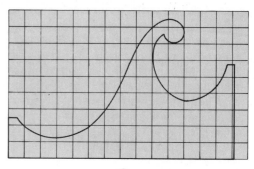

Part ④ Detail

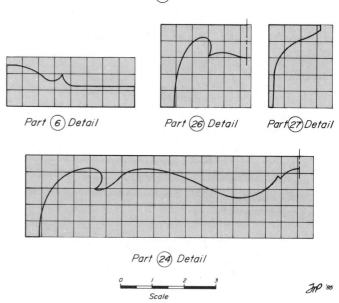

Part ⑥ Detail   Part ㉖ Detail   Part㉗Detail

Part ㉔ Detail

help stabilize the work. It is best to finish sanding the columns and apply a coat of filler to them while they are in the lathe.

Door

The clock door is made from 1 1/4" wide walnut strips. It is important that the door pieces be warp-free. You may find that you will need to cull out several pieces to get long warp-free pieces. The door frame parts 15, 16, 17 & 18 are inlaid with a tiny band of 1/28" holly. This detail is optional and was not found on originals. If you opt for inlay, it is easier to inlay the door parts before mitering. I cut the inlay slots with a Dremel tool 3/16" from the door's edge and 1/16" deep and glue in strips of 1/28" holly veneer. Miter the frame pieces, cut the half lap joint, and fit the sash. Make a trial fit on all door joints to check for squareness. After the door joints are fitted, apply glue to all joints and clamp. I use a rubber

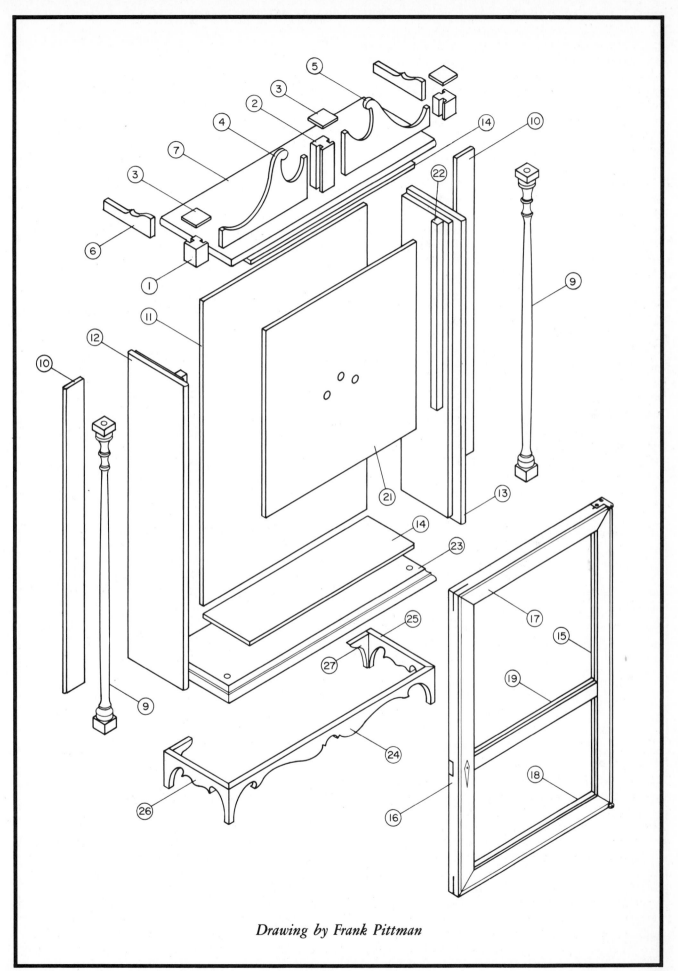

Drawing by Frank Pittman

band made from bicycle inner tube as a clamp to hold the mitered frame together. This assembly should be allowed to dry overnight. Feather slots are cut across each miter joint using a table saw set up similar to the one shown in *The American Woodworker*, June 1985. Oversize feathers are glued in the kerfs and allowed to dry. The feathers are later trimmed flush with the door frame.

A portable router and router table can be used to form the rabbet around the door frame for the glass. This procedure leaves a radius in each corner which must be squared out by hand.

Hinges for the door, as shown in the drawing detail, are made from 1/16″ brass stock with a #2 x 3/8″ round head screw serving as a pivot. Gains for the hinges can be cut in the door frame by hand or with a Dremel tool.

Original Terry clocks used a special eccentric brass door catch. A catch such as this can be obtained from Ball and Ball, 463 West Lincoln Highway, Exton, PA 19341. I opted for a small magnetic catch instead. The small magnet is located in the case side behind the door sash. A small flat head steel screw in the door is used as the striker plate for the magnet.

The diamond shaped inlay piece for the door can be cut from holly or maple veneer. I usually center this inlay next to the door sash and cut the recess with a Dremel tool. On original clocks this diamond was frequently centered on the door side, not the sash. The door pull should be brass and "key like". I have actually made pulls from small brass door keys or brass lamp knobs.

The back of the case and the movement mount can be made from 1/4″ plywood. I use birch plywood stained walnut or walnut veneer plywood.

Assembly and Finishing:

It is best to sand all parts through 220 and paste fill before assembly. I use a #674 brown paster filler for walnut that I obtain from Grand Rapids Finishing Co., 53-71 Grandville Ave. S. W., Grand Rapids, MI 49502. After the filler has dried, assemble all parts. I use a lacquer finish on the case rubbed to a satin sheen with 0000 steel wool.

"An important first step in clock making is to obtain the movement, face, and related hardware."

Movement and Chime Installation

The type of movement will determine the actual installation needs. I have used both 1/2 hour strike and Westminster chime movements in this clock (Mason & Sullivan #3350X or #3354X). The movement is screwed to the 1/4″ dial mounting board. A separate mounting board is usually necessary for the chimes. Movement installation should begin with the clock face as a reference. The dial should be 12 3/8″ x 12 3/8″ with a 9 1/2″ time ring. First, center the clock face in the upper part of the door and mark the location of the face holes in the plywood mounting board (part #21). Drill these holes slightly oversize. Next, center the movement over the holes and screw it in place. It is important that the winding stems of the movement center themselves in the clock face holes.

Door glass should be installed after finishing. Use small #2 x 1/4″ flat head brass screws or brads in the retainer strips.

BILL OF MATERIALS					
Item	Description	QTY	T	W	L
1	Pedestal	2	1″ x	1″ x	1 1/4″
2	Center Pedestal	1	1″ x	1″ x	2 7/8″
3	Pedestal Cap	3	1/8″ x	1 3/16″ x	1 3/16″
4-5	Broken Pediment	2	5/16″ x	4 1/4″ x	7 1/16″
6	Crown Side	2	5/16″ x	1 1/4″ x	4″
7	Crown Base	1	7/16″ x	5 3/16″ x	16 5/8″
8	V-blocks	1	3/8″ x	3/8″ x	22″
9	Columns	2	1″ x	1″ x	21 1/8″
10	Back Fins	2	1/4″ x	1 1/2″ x	21 1/8″
11	Plywood Back	1	1/4″ x	13 1/4″ x	21 1/8″
12-13	Sides	2	3/4″ x	4 11/16″ x	21 1/8″
14	Inner top & bottom	2	1/4″ x	3 7/8″ x	13 1/4″
15-16	Door Sides	2	23/32″ x	1 1/4″ x	21″
17-18	Door top & bottom	2	23/32″ x	1 1/4″ x	13 1/8″
19	Sash	1	23/32″ x	15/16″ x	13 1/8″
20	Glass Retainer	1	1/8″ x	3/8″ x	91″
21	Dial Mount (Plywood)	1	1/4″ x	12 3/4″ x	13″
22	Dial Mount Blocks	2	1/2″ x	1/2″ x	13″
23	Base	1	3/4″ x	5 1/2″ x	17 3/8″
24	Front Foot	1	3/8″ x	2 1/2″ x	17 1/8″
25-26	Side Foot	2	3/8″ x	2 1/2″ x	5 3/8″
27	Back Foot	2	3/8″ x	1 5/8″ x	2 1/2″

ABOUT THE AUTHOR
Frank Pittman is the Graphic Drawing Editor for **The American Woodworker.**

A LANTERN STYLE VIENNA REGULATOR WALL CLOCK

BY FRANK M. PITTMAN

*Photos by
Marshall Love
Studios*

Clocks known today as Vienna Regulators were produced mainly in Vienna, Austria from approximately 1800 to 1900. The first regulators were made during the latter part of the Empire period or about 1804-1814. The clock case in this article is patterned after a type known as Laterndluhr in Vienna (circa 1810-1820) and has glass on three sides, resembling a lantern. This case was designed around a two weight Kieninger movement with a 7″ dial and a 26″ pendulum. (The pendulum length is measured from the center of the dial to the end of the stick.) This movement, model M352, was acquired from the Ramcraft Clock Company, 331 W. Eastland, Gallatin, Tennessee 37066. Other movements could be used, but the entire case must be designed accordingly. Items such as movement depth, dial diameter, width required for weight drop, pendulum length, and pendulum swing are all important design considerations.

Original lantern style cases were usually made from either mahogany, rosewood, walnut, or maple with fancy veneers and satinwood inlay being common. The clock pictured here was made from American black walnut with holly inlay.

BASE CONSTRUCTION

Case construction can actually begin on either the hood, waist, or base, but I will begin the explanation with the base and go up.

It is best to make part number 4 (base) from quarter sawn stock to minimize warping. Wide quarter sawn pieces are rare, but it can be made from several narrow quartered strips glued together. The large base molding (part #3) presents an interesting problem and several different methods of fabrication could be used. After looking at some old clocks and talking to a clock collecting friend of mine, I decided to make this part from solid stock, band sawing and sanding. If you are lucky enough to have some 4″ thick walnut stock, you could use it here. I glued two 8/4 pieces together to form the 3½″ x 5½″ x 9 1/8″ finished blank.

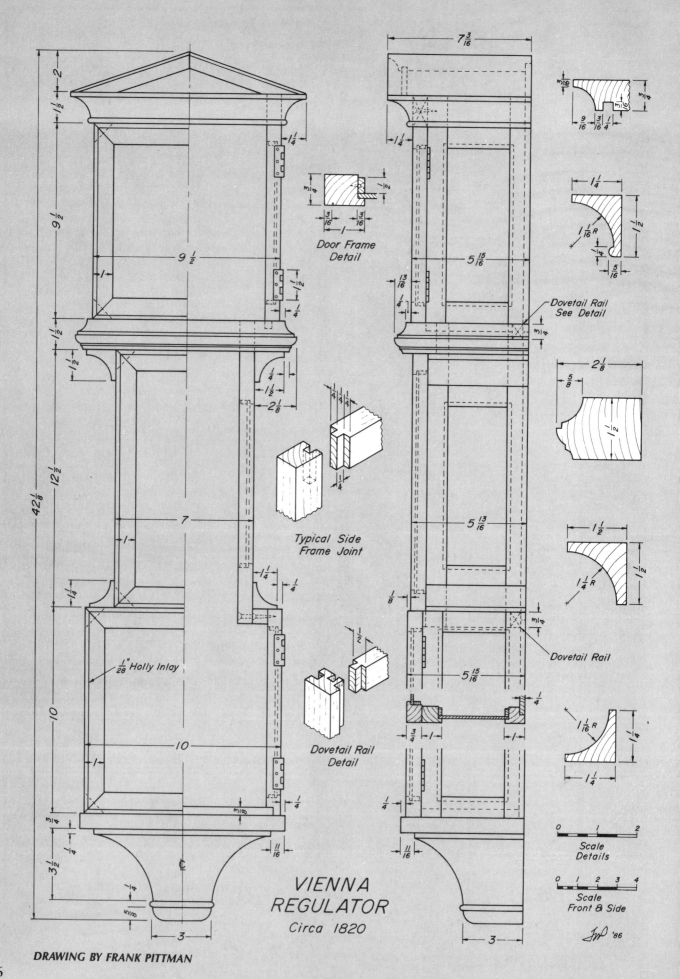

Door Frame
Detail

Typical Side
Frame Joint

Dovetail Rail
See Detail

Dovetail Rail

Dovetail Rail
Detail

$\frac{1}{28}$" Holly Inlay

VIENNA
REGULATOR
Circa 1820

Scale
Details

Scale
Front & Side

DRAWING BY FRANK PITTMAN

Square the blank carefully and then layout and cut the coves on a bandsaw. If you don't have a band saw with a 9″ capacity under the upper guide, you could form the cove by sawing or planing off the waste stock by hand and then hand carve and scrape to final shape. After sanding the molding through 220 grit, parts #1 and #2 can be made and glued to the bottom.

The entire case involves a large number of ¾″ x 1″ strips for the sides and doors. it is best to prepare all of this stock at one time. Approximately 24 feet of ¾″ x 1″ material is required for the entire project; however, you should prepare several extra pieces to provide a choice later. Some of the strips will probably reject themselves due to warping and other defects.

The base side frames are joined together with mortise and tenon joints. The rabbet for the back can be cut before or after assembly. The rabbet for the glass and the inner bottom should be cut after assembly. You can use a portable router with a router table to cut the glass rabbet and a table saw to cut the inner bottom rabbet.

The spacers for the top of the base (part #17) can be cut and attached to the top of the base with #8, 1¼″ flat head screws. The inner bottom can be prepared from 3/8″ material.

WAIST SIDES

The sides of the waist are fabricated like the base sides. A single female dovetail cut is made in the top and bottom of the rear frame pieces. This dovetail cut can be made using a small dovetail router bit and router table. The waist moldings (parts #33, 34, 35, 36) can be cut on a table saw using a core box sawing technique. The dovetail rails (parts #19 & 32) should be made to fit into the side frames.

HOOD

The foundation for the hood is the "U" shaped molding formed from parts #37, 38, and 39. This molding was made from 8/4 stock, however, it could be

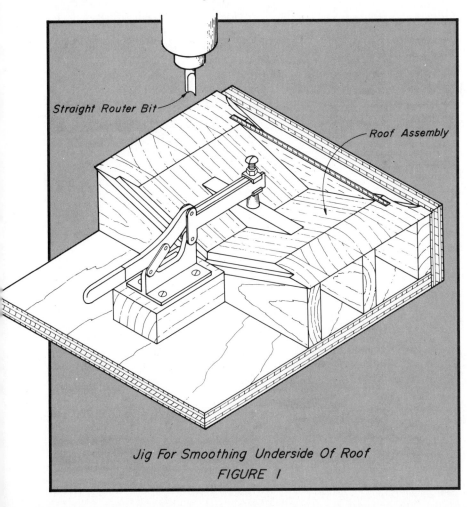

Straight Router Bit

Roof Assembly

Jig For Smoothing Underside Of Roof
FIGURE 1

formed by stacking thinner pieces together. A router or shaper can be used to form this molding. The molding is mitered on each corner and the miter is reinforced with a blind spline. You should cut 3/8″ x ½″ grooves in each of the side moldings before gluing the miters together.

The hood sides are fabricated like the base and waist sides, cutting the rabbet for the lower tongue and groove joint after assembly.

I made a special shaper cutter to produce the upper hood molding (parts #52, 53, and 54). You could also produce it by cutting the cove on a table saw using a core box technique and then glue a small bead molding to the bottom edge.

All hood parts should be sanded through 220 grit before assembly. Hood assembly involves gluing the base molding together, gluing the sides to the molding assembly, attaching the hood front spacer (part #55), and then gluing on the upper hood molding.

The top of the hood (parts #57 and 58) presented another interesting challenge. I considered a number of different options before finally deciding to make it from ¾″ solid stock. If you opt for this procedure select the stock carefully. Quarter sawn material is best to minimize warping and expansion and contraction problems. I actually glued several 2″ wide quartered strips together to form a top blank, approximately ¾″ x 7 3/16″ x 16″. A cove molding is cut on the front edge of the blank and a ¼″ x 3/8″ rabbet is cut on the back. A ¼″ x 3/16″ groove is cut near the cove for part #57. The center 18½ degree miter can be cut on a table saw. A blind spline cut is made across the miter using a router table, a 1/8″ splining bit and a special jig to hold the part at the proper angle. Fabricate a cross-grain spline 1/8″ x ½″ x 7″ then glue the spline mitered pieces together. While this assembly is drying the triangular gable front piece can be prepared. This piece looks best if it is veneered with a highly figured wood. I used burl walnut veneer glued to a piece of ¼″ plywood. After the veneer assembly is dry, the triangular shape can be cut out and the part can be sanded and glued into the groove in the roof.

The long angle cuts at the base of the roof are next. A jig can be used to hold the assembly on edge and make the rough angle cuts on a band saw. The rough band sawn surface produced with this technique must be smoothed to form a good fit between the roof and the top hood molding. Smoothing can be done with a hand plane, however, I used a jig, like the one shown in Figure 1, and an over-arm pin router with a straight bit to flatten these surfaces. If you do not have access to a pin router, a high speed drill press could be used in the same way. The flattening operation should continue until the surfaces are smooth and the part is approximately 12¼″ long. At this point the roof should overhang the top molding approximately 1/8″. The cove molding on the front of the roof gable end should be sanded through 220 grit, and after sanding, the roof assembly can be glued to the top hood molding. Small spring clamps can be used to help hold the assembly in place while the glue dries. After drying the 1/8″ overhang can be planed and sanded off flush with the hood molding.

ASSEMBLY
(Base, Waist, and Hood)

The overall assembly of the base, waist, and hood must be carefully planned. You may discover a better way, but I used the following procedure: locate, drill, and countersink all shank holes for screws; the anchor holes are drilled during assembly. You will find that there are times during assembly when the space is too limited to permit the use of conventional drills when making the anchor holes. A pin vise equipped with a small twist drill can be used when this happens.

First, screw the base sides to the waist sides being certain that the back edges of both assemblies are aligned. Next, install the inner bottom with #5 x 5/8″ screws and glue the upper and lower dovetail rails into the waist sides. Now, the waist sides can be screwed to the inside of the hood base molding. This is a place where a pin vise is necessary for drilling the anchor holes for the screws. During the entire assembly process, be sure that all components are square. It is best to screw the assemblies together first and check for squareness and then disassemble, apply glue and reassemble. The large base molding can be screwed and glued to the inner bottom using #5 x ¾″ screws.

DOORS

The clock doors are fabricated from ¾″ x 1″ material with feathered mitered corners. The door parts should be inlaid with 1/28″ holly strips and rabbeted with a 3/16″ x 9/16″ glass rabbet before mitering. A modified Dremel cutter, router, and router table were used to cut the inlay grooves. Locate these grooves approximately 3/16″ from the outer edge of the pieces. The glass rabbet can be cut using a router, table saw, or shaper. The mitered frames are butt glued using a heavy rubber band as a clamp. The rubber band can be made from an old bicycle inner tube. The saw cuts for the feathers can be cut across the miters after the frames have dried using a jig on the table saw similar to the one shown in *The American Woodworker*, June 1985. Feathers can now be fabricated and glued in each miter.

I opted not to hinge the waist door and simply butt glued it to the front edge of the waist sides. The hood and base doors are hinged using 1½″ brass butt hinges. A small round magnetic catch was used on each door, with the magnet being installed in the case side and the striker plate on the door. No door pull is used since the doors can be opened by simply pulling on the door's edge.

BACK

The back of the clock is quite visible and should be made from solid walnut or walnut veneer plywood. Make the back in three pieces, one for the base, waist, and hood respectively. Shank holes can be drilled and countersunk in the back pieces for #5 x 5/8″ flat head screws. The hood back also serves as a mounting board for the movement and chime so mounting holes for these parts must be carefully located and drilled. It is important when locating the movement that the dial be centered in the hood door.

Figure 2

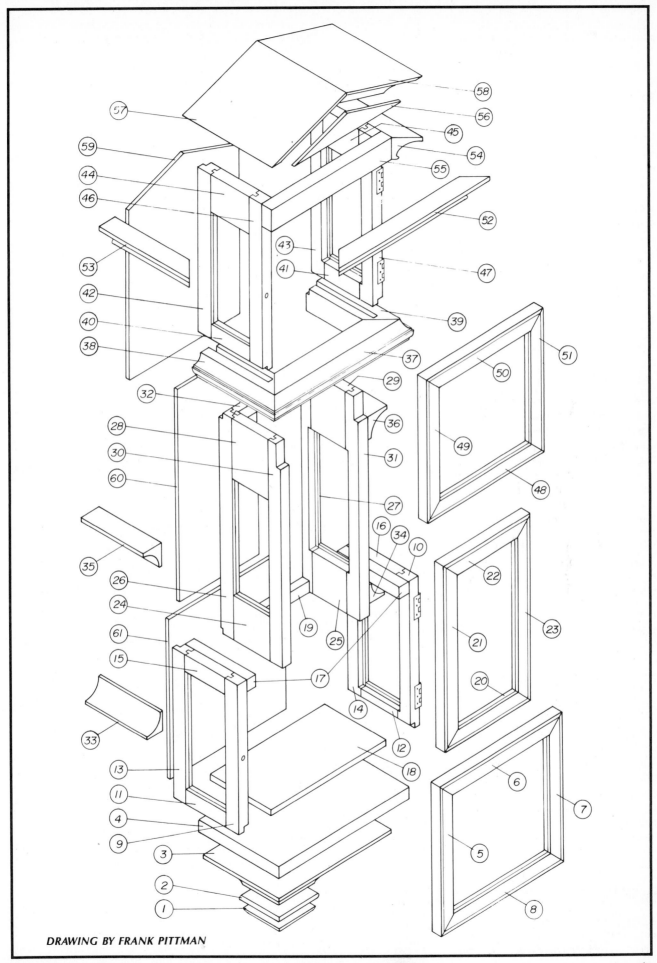

DRAWING BY FRANK PITTMAN

Provisions for hanging the clock need to be made in the hood back. I used the system shown in the photograph, Figure 2.

FINISHING

Glass retainer strips, 1/8″ x 3/8″ should be cut for each side and door frame. These pieces should be mitered, drilled, countersunk and sanded. The entire clock should be finished sanded inside and out through 220 grit. I used a brown paste filler and lacquer finish. Rub the final coat of lacquer with 0000 steel wool to produce a satin sheen.

After all parts have been rubbed down, the glass can be installed. I have found it is easier to take my clocks to a glass company and have them cut glass to fit each opening. It is best to do this before the clock is finished to avoid possible damage to the finished parts.

Clean each glass panel well before installation to simplify the final clean up. Use #2 x 3/8″ flat head brass screws to install the glass. A pin vise and a small twist drill can be used to drill the anchor holes for these screws. After the glass is installed, the movement and chimes are mounted to the hood back, and the backs can be screwed in place.

The clock can be hung from a single heavy screw at the top. Let it run for a few weeks, adjusting the pendulum length and case location until it keeps good time and is "in beat". A small screw can then be installed through the base back into the wall to keep the case from moving from side to side. This screw can be located behind the regulator plate.

The clean, simple classical lines of this clock make it blend well into a variety of decorator settings ranging from period to modern. It is truly a versatile design.

REFERENCE:
Ortenburger, Rick, Viennese Regulators **and Industrialized Clock Factories,** *1981, Pendel Uhr Publications, Agoura, California.*

ABOUT THE AUTHOR:
Frank Pittman is the graphic drawing editor for The American Woodworker.

70

BILL OF MATERIAL

CODE	DESCRIPTION	QUAN	T	W	L
1	Base cap	1	5/8″	3″	3″
2	Bead	1	¼″	3¼″	3¼″
3	Base molding	1	3½″	5½″	9 1/8″
4	Base	1	¾″	6 3/16″	10½″
5, 7	Lower door stile	2	¾″	1″	10″
6, 8	Lower door rail	2	¾″	1″	10″
9, 10	Frame, base	2	¾″	1″	10″
11, 12	Frame, base	2	¾″	1″	3 5/8″
13, 14	Frame, base	2	¾″	1″	10″
15, 16	Frame, base	2	¾″	1″	3 5/8″
17	Spacer	2	¾″	¾″	4 15/16″
18	Inner bottom	1	3/8″	4 15/16″	9¼″
19	Dovetail rail	1	½″	¾″	6″
20, 22	Waist door rail	2	¾″	1″	7″
21, 23	Waist door stile	2	¾″	1″	12½″
24, 25	Frame, waist	2	¾″	3″	3½″
26, 27	Frame, waist	2	¾″	1″	14¾″
28, 29	Frame, waist	2	¾″	4″	3½″
30, 31	Frame, waist	2	¾″	1″	14¾″
32	Dovetail rail	1	½″	¾″	6″
33, 34	Molding	2	1¼″	1¼″	5 1/16″
35, 36	Molding	2	1½″	1½″	5 1/16″
37	Hood base molding	1	1½″	2 1/8″	11¼″
38, 39	Hood base molding	2	1½″	2 1/8″	6¾″
40, 41	Frame, hood	2	¾″	1 3/8″	3 5/8″
42, 43	Frame, hood	2	¾″	1″	11 3/8″
44, 45	Frame, hood	2	¾″	2½″	3 5/8″
46, 47	Frame, hood	2	¾″	1″	11 3/8″
48, 50	Hood door rail	2	¾″	1″	9½″
49, 51	Hood door stile	2	¾″	1″	9½″
52	Molding	1	1½″	1¼″	12″
53, 54	Molding	2	1½″	1¼″	7 3/16″
55	Spacer	1	¾″	1½″	9½″
56	Gable front	1	¼″	2″	9″
57, 58	Top	2	¾″	7 3/16″	7″
59	Hood back	1	¼″	8¾″	13″
60	Waist back	1	¼″	6¼″	14″
61	Base back	1	¼″	9¼″	9 5/8″

DUTCH CUPBOARD

by Franklin H. Gottshall

Large cupboards, like the one shown here, are to be found in homes of people in Pennsylvania counties like Berks, Lehigh, Montgomery, and Lancaster. Early immigrants from Germany and Switzerland were encouraged to settle in this area by William Penn, and these came to be known as the ''Pennsylvania Dutch,'' due to the similarity of the words ''Dutch,'' and ''Deutsch,'' which is the term by which the German language is known in Germany. To a German, Germany is Deutschland.

Cupboards of various sizes, with glazed doors to display collections of china are to be found in many homes in southeastern Pennsylvania. While most are smaller in size than this one, it is not unusual to find examples like this built to display large collections of treasured antiques.

To build the cupboard, start by building the lower section first. The wood used to build the cupboard shown was cherry, with poplar used as a secondary wood for shelves, floors, drawer sides and backs, and hidden members that do not show.

Cut stock for both ends (A), stiles (C) and (D), rails (E), (F) and (H), and stiles (G). Ends are wide enough so it is advisable to glue several narrower boards edge-to-edge to attain the width needed. Lumber thick enough to retain thicknesses of 7/8″ after gluing, planing, and sanding have been done on them, should be used. Achieve proper thicknesses first, then exact widths and lengths.

The floor and the cupboard ceiling should be made next. Preferably poplar should be used to make these, though pine could be an acceptable substitute. When these have been dressed to size, lay out and cut grooves on the inside of both ends to hold them as shown in Figure 4. Back edges of both ends (A) should be rabbeted to provide places to nail fast the plywood back so it will not be visible on the outside. Once this has been done, ends (A), ceiling (T), and floor (U) may be glued together.

Make the front next. This consists of stiles (C) and (D), rails (E), (F), (H), and stiles (G). Lay out and cut mortise-and-tenon joints on these, as shown in Figure 4; then glue these parts together. Heads of finish nails, used to nail front to ends, should be hidden as much as possible under moldings which will be applied later. Glue may be used to fasten rail (F) to the edge of ceiling (T). When quarter columns are glued to outside corners, it will help hold front and ends together.

Make drawer runs (V), and drawer guides (X) and (W), and fasten them with wood screws to the top of the cupboard ceiling.

Make the front and back feet. Details for making these are shown in Figures 6 and 7. Fasten these to the bottom of the floor. Feet (I) and (J) may be roughly shaped on the outside on the table saw, and then smoothed with chisel, file, and sandpaper. Cut and glue the miter joints on the front feet, and cut rabbets on top to fasten the triangular pieces (Z-1) and (Z-2). These triangular-shaped blocks may then be screwed fast to the underside of the floor to hold the front feet in place.

When front and back feet have been fastened to the bottom, the drawers should be made and fitted next. Details to make the drawers are shown in Figure 8. Dovetails on drawer sides may be cut to shape on the band saw. Then, placing these over ends of drawer fronts and drawer backs, trace the outlines of the tails, to get the outlines of the

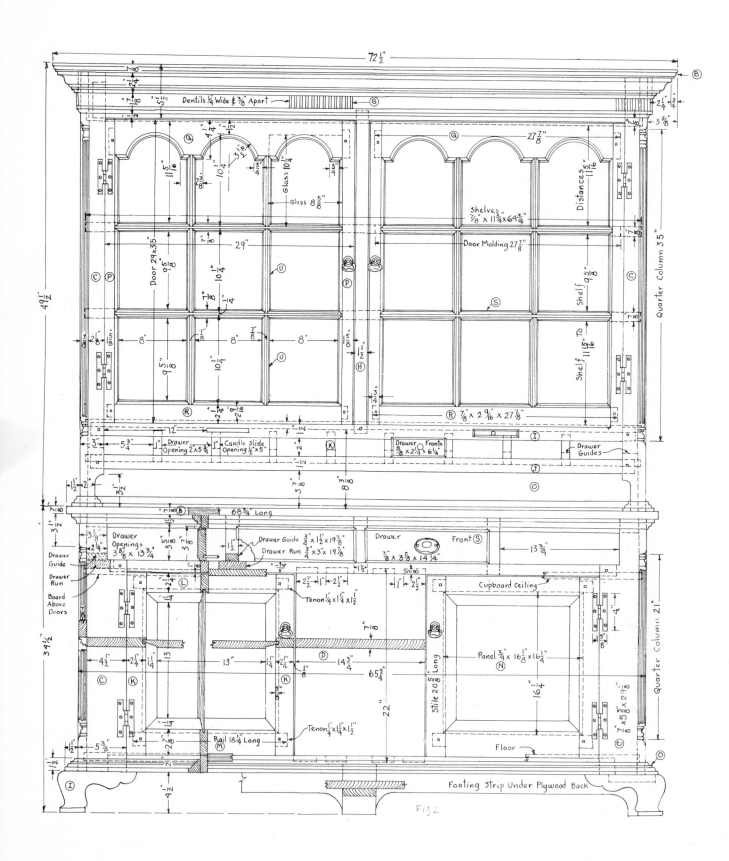

Fig 2

pin members. On the drawer backs, most of the waste around the dovetail pins can be removed by first outlining the pins with saw kerfs made with a hand dovetail saw, and then removing most of the waste in between these saw cuts with parallel band saw cuts. These band saw cuts must, however, be made with the inside surface of the drawer back facing up. The small amount of waste still left after this has been done may then be removed with a coping saw. *(See Vol I, No. I., Ed.)*

On the drawer fronts, outline the pins with the hand dovetail saw. This can be done if the drawer front is held in a vise with the inside of the drawer front facing you, and with the end being worked on top. The waste to be removed after this has been done must be chiseled out. Grooves to hold the drawer bottoms may be made on the circular saw. When assembling the drawers, glue the dovetail joints, but do not glue drawer bottoms to the grooves which hold them.

Make the doors. Dimensions and details to make the doors are found in Figure 2. Make grooves and mortises first; then fit tenons and panels to them. Make the panels before gluing rails and stiles together. Panels are not glued to the grooves which hold them and their width is 1/8″ less than their height to permit some swelling during damp seasons of the year. Hinges, and other hardware sizes and shapes, are shown in Figures 2 and 10.

Make and fasten the top (B) next. Strips of wood, fastened with wood screws to the under side of the top, and then to rail (E), and ends (A), hold the top in place, and it is held in place in back when the plywood back is nailed to its back edge there.

The molding around the bottom, above the feet, and under the top should now be made and fastened. It may be held in place with brads and glue on front, but only brads should be used to fasten it to ends (A). The miter joints at both front corners should be glued.

Make the upper section. Ends (A) of the upper section are only 12″ wide, and if stock this wide is available, gluing together of narrower pieces need not be done. Cut, plane, and sand stock for these, and for end stiles (C), top rail (D), rails (I) and (J), and stiles (H) and (K). Saw stiles (C) to shape on the band saw, as shown in Figures 2 and 11. When all of the above have been made to the sizes given in the Bill of Material, lay out, cut and fit mortise-and-tenon joints on pieces (C), (D), (H), (I), (J), and (K).

Make the ceiling board and the four shelves; then lay out and cut grooves in ends (A) to hold these. Rabbet back edges of ends (A) to fasten the plywood back. Make holder supports (Y) and fasten them with wood screws under the second shelf from the bottom. Make the ten drawer guides and fasten them with screws to the top of the shelf under the small drawers. Then glue shelves and ceiling board to ends (A).

Glue up the front frame, consisting of stiles (C), (H), and (K) to rails (D), (I), and (J). Nail the frame to ends (A), hiding nail heads under where frieze (E) and moldings will cover them. Stiles (C) may be glued to ends (A) above and below the quarter columns. When the quarter columns have been made, they should be glued to the front edges of (A) and the glued-up frame.

Make the frieze (E) and (F). Dentils 1/8″ thick and

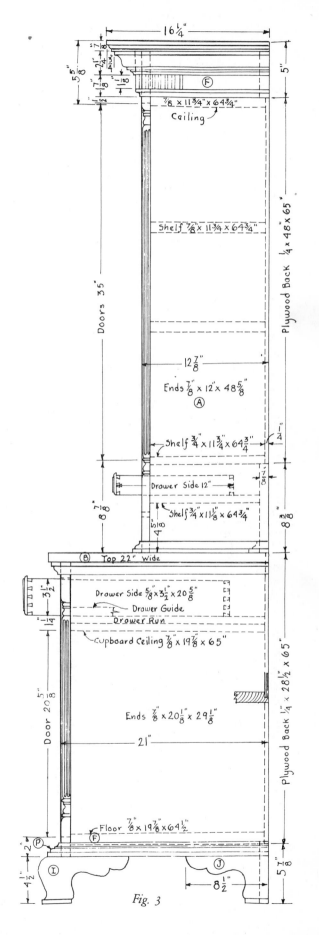

Fig. 3

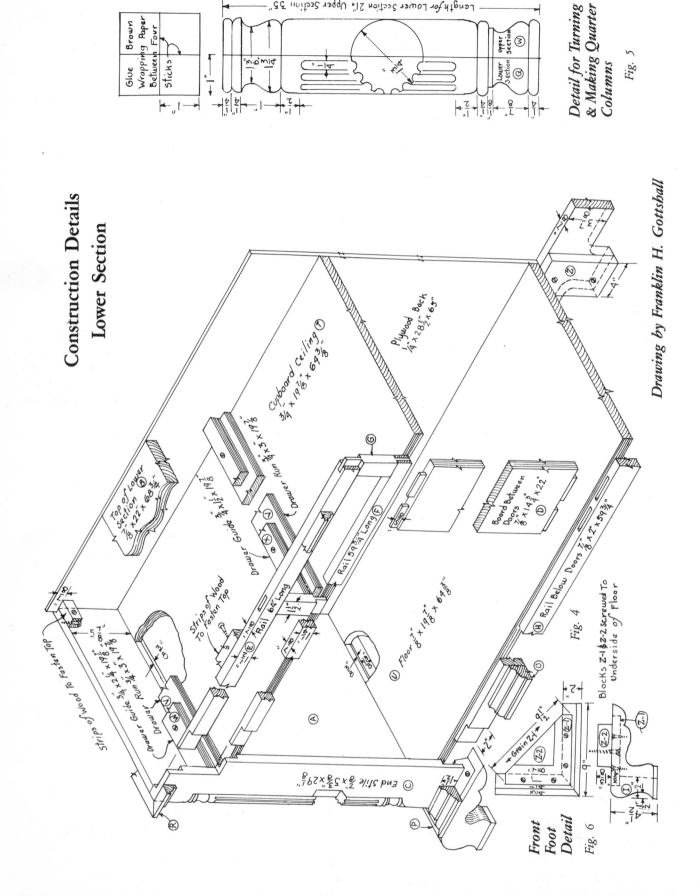

Construction Details
Lower Section

Detail for Turning & Making Quarter Columns

Fig. 5

Drawing by Franklin H. Gottshall

Glue Brown Wrapping Paper Between Four Sticks

Length for Lower Section 21½ Upper Section 35″

Upper Section W

Lower Section G

Top of Lower Section ⅞″ x 22 x 63¾″

Cupboard Ceiling T ¾ x 19⅞ x 64⅜″

Drawer Run ¾ x 3 x 19⅞

Drawer Guide ¾ x 1½ x 19⅞

Strips of Wood To Fasten Top

Drawer Guide ¾ x 2¼ x 19⅞

Rail 64″ Long E

Rail 59¾ Long F

Floor ⅞ x 19⅞ x 64⅜″ U

Plywood Back ¼″ x 28½ x 65″

Board Between Doors ⅞ x 14¾ x 22″ D

Rail Below Doors ⅞ x 2 x 59¾ H

Drawer Guide ¾″ x 2¼ x 19⅞

Drawer Run ¾ x 3 x 19⅞

Strips of Wood to Fasten Top

End Stile ⅞ x 5⅜ x 29¼″ C

Fig. 4

Blocks Z-1 & Z-2 screwed To Underside of Floor

Grain Z-1

Z-2

Z-1

Z-2

Front Foot Detail

Fig. 6

1/4″ wide are spaced 3/8″ apart on the lower edge of the frieze and are glued to it below the cornice molding.

Make and fit doors and drawers before making and fastening top and moldings. The smaller drawers in the upper section are made of thinner stock than those in the lower section, but the same procedure for making and fitting them applies. Make trial assemblies without gluing joints to be sure each drawer moves back and forth freely in its opening. Make and assemble the upper section doors. Enough muntin molding should be made on a shaper to make all the rails and stiles needed for both

---

"...Cupboards of various sizes, with glazed doors to display collections of china, are to be found in many homes in southeastern Pennsylvania."

---

doors. If a shaper is not part of the equipment in your workshop, the nearest planing mill can do this shaping for you. Rails (Q) and (R), and stiles (P) should all be made and cut to size and shape, and the molding on all cut at the same time. All pieces used to make a door should be glued where they are joined to each other.

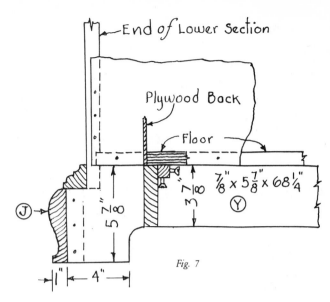

Fig. 7

Construction at Bottom in Back

When the doors and drawers have been made and fitted into place, the top (B) should be made and nailed to ends (A), and to rails (D) and (Z). Then make and fasten crown molding (V), and the 1″ molding around the ends and the inside of the bottom. The plywood back may then be nailed fast.

The upper section is not fastened to the top of the lower section but merely rests upon it.

The inside of the upper section is painted white, or

Drawer Construction
In Lower Section

Fig.8

Fig.8

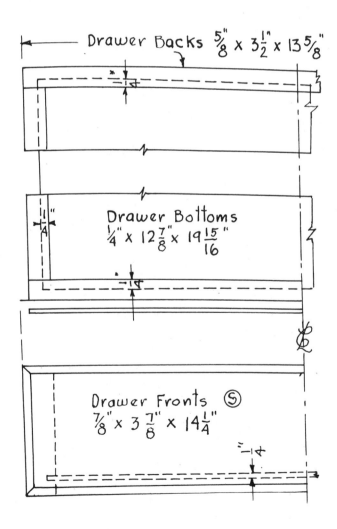

Drawer Backs $\frac{5}{8}$″ x $3\frac{1}{2}$″ x $13\frac{5}{8}$″

Drawer Bottoms $\frac{1}{4}$″ x $12\frac{7}{8}$″ x $19\frac{15}{16}$″

Drawer Fronts ⓢ
$\frac{7}{8}$″ x $3\frac{7}{8}$″ x $14\frac{1}{4}$″

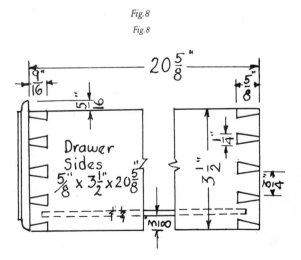

Drawer Sides $\frac{5}{8}$″ x $3\frac{1}{2}$″ x $20\frac{5}{8}$″

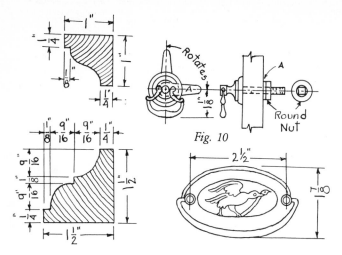

Molding Details

Fig. 9

Fig. 10

a light-hued pastel semi-gloss color. The outside of this cupboard was stained with oil stain, wiped dry as possible with cotton cloths immediately following application. When this had dried several days, several finishing coats of glossy floor varnish were applied over the stain. Each finishing coat, after being allowed to dry thoroughly, was rubbed down with fine-grit open-coat garnet paper and #0 steel wool before the next coat was applied. Dust from this smoothing down process must be carefully removed before succeeding coats are applied, and finishing coats should only be put on in a dry dust-free room. The final coat was rubbed down with felt pads and clean cotton cloths dipped in powdered pumice stone and furniture rubbing oil.

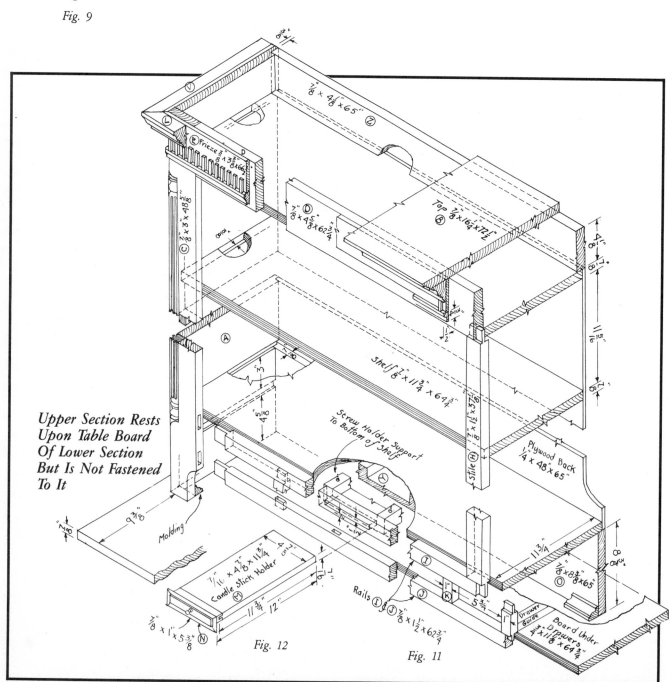

Upper Section Rests Upon Table Board Of Lower Section But Is Not Fastened To It

Fig. 12

Fig. 11

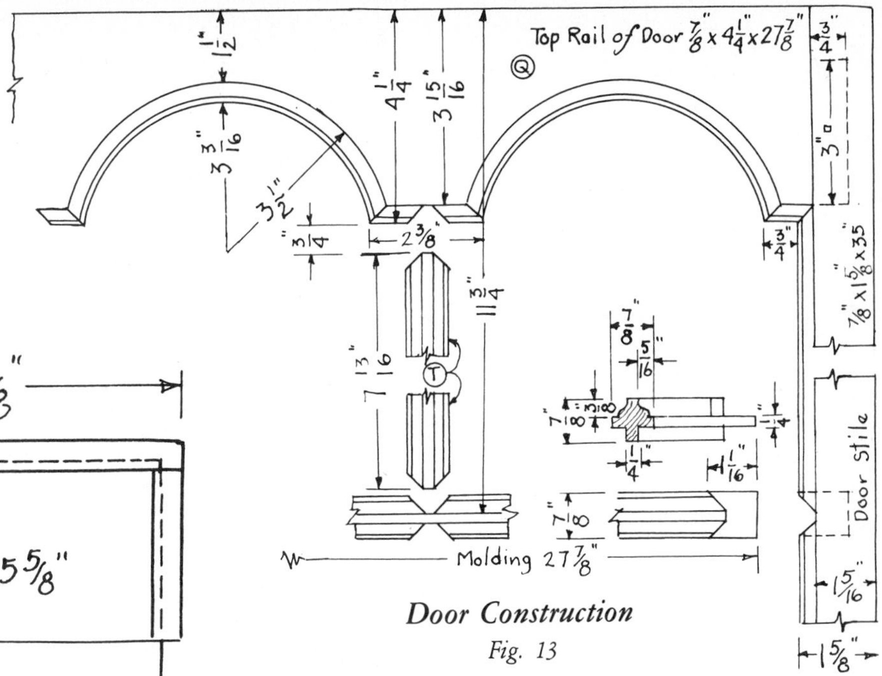
Top Rail of Door 7/8" x 4 1/4" x 27 7/8"
Q
T
Molding 27 7/8"
Door Stile
7/8" x 1 5/8" x 35"

Door Construction

Fig. 13

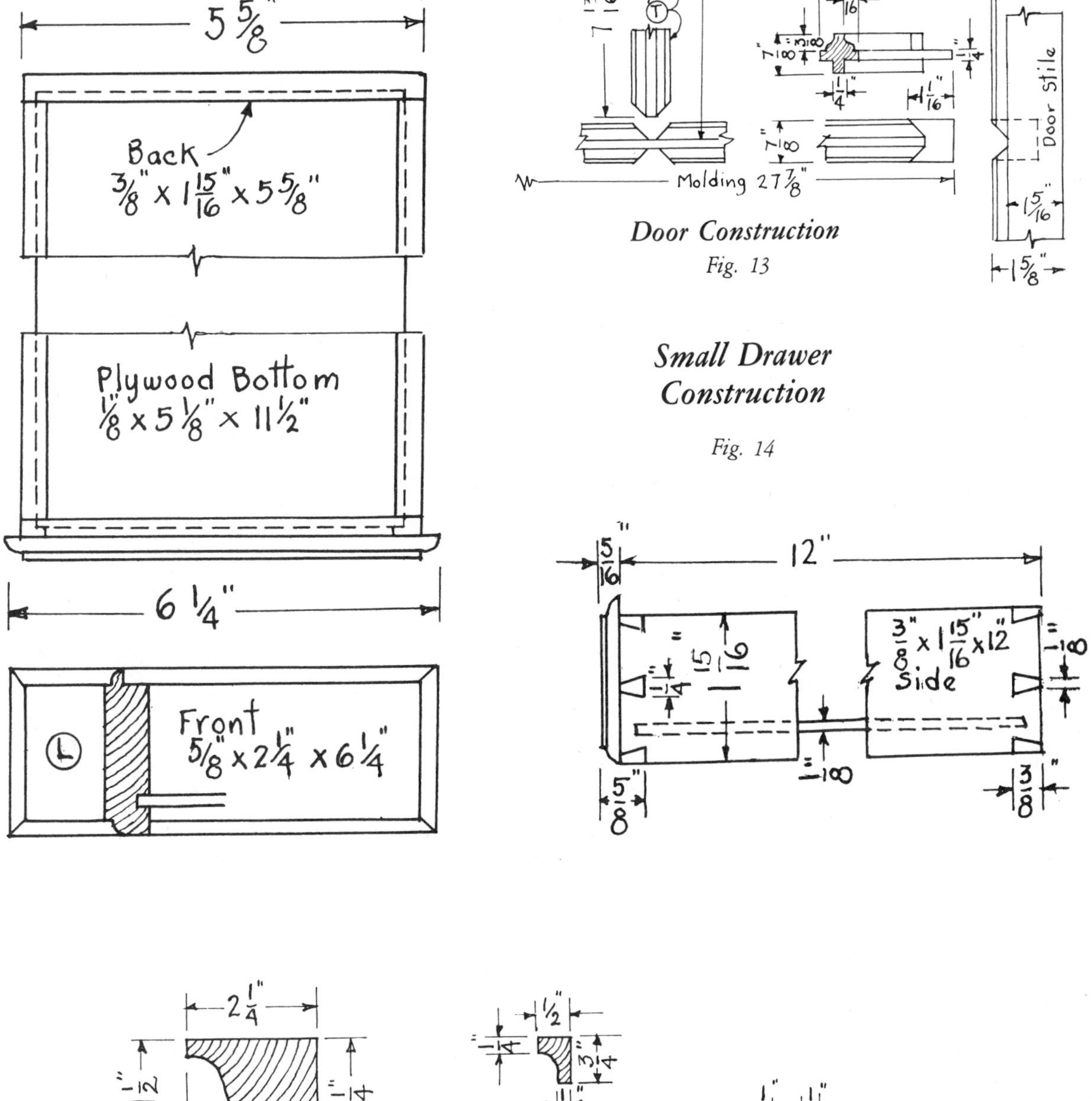
5 5/8"
Back 3/8" x 1 15/16" x 5 5/8"
Plywood Bottom 1/8" x 5 1/8" x 11 1/2"
6 1/4"
L
Front 5/8" x 2 1/4" x 6 1/4"
12"
3/8" x 1 15/16" x 12"
Side

Small Drawer Construction

Fig. 14

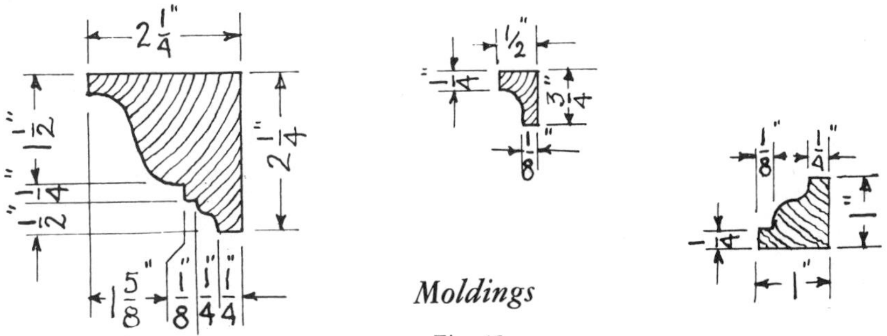

Moldings

Fig. 15

Drawing by Franklin H. Gottshall

BILL OF MATERIALS

LOWER SECTION
CHERRY

(A) 2 ends 7/8″ x 20 1/8″ x 29 1/8″

(B) 1 top 7/8″ x 22″ x 68 3/4″

(C) 2 end stiles 7/8″ x 5 3/8″ x 29 1/8″

(D) 1 board between doors 7/8″ x 14 3/4″ x 22″

(E) 1 rail above drawers 7/8″ x 1 1/2″ x 64″

(F) 1 rail below drawers 7/8″ x 1 1/4″ x 59 3/4″

(G) 3 stiles between drawers 7/8″ x 1 1/2″ x 6 3/8″

(H) 1 rail below doors 7/8″ x 2″ x 59 3/4″

(I) front feet, 4 pcs. 2″ x 4 1/2″ x 9″

(J) back feet, 2 pcs. 2″ x 4 1/2″ x 8 1/2″

(K) 4 door stiles 7/8″ x 2 1/4″ x 20 5/8″

(L) 2 top door rails 7/8″ x 2 1/4″ x 18 1/4″

(M) 2 bottom door rails 7/8″ x 2 7/8″ x 18 1/4″

(N) 2 door panels 3/4″ x 16 1/8″ x 16 1/4″

(O) molding above feet, 1 pc. 1 1/2″ x 1 1/2″ x 68 3/4″

(P) molding above feet, 2 pcs. 1 1/2″ x 1 1/2″ x 22 1/2″

(Q) quarter columns (lower section) 4 pcs. 1″ x 1″ x 21″

(R) molding under top, 1 pc. (front and ends) 1″ x 1″ x 114″

(S) 4 drawer fronts 7/8″ x 3 7/8″ x 14 1/4″

POPLAR

(T) 1 cupboard ceiling 3/4″ x 19 7/8″ x 64 3/8″

(U) 1 cupboard floor 7/8″ x 19 7/8″ x 64 3/8″

(V) 5 drawer runs 3/4″ x 3″ x 19 7/8″

(W) 2 drawer guides 3/4″ x 2 1/4″ x 19 7/8″

(X) 3 drawer guides 3/4″ x 1 1/2″ x 19 7/8″

(Y) 1 rail between back feet 7/8″ x 5 7/8″ x 68 1/4″

(Z) 1 reinforcing block inside back foot rail 7/8″ x 4″ x 5 7/8″

(Z1) 2 triangular pcs., top of front feet 3/4″ x 4 1/4″ x 9 1/2″

(Z2) 2 triangular blocks, top of front feet 1 3/8″ x 3″ x 6″

8 drawer sides 5/8″ x 3 1/2″ x 20 5/8″

4 drawer backs 5/8″ x 3 1/2″ x 13 5/8″

BIRCH PLYWOOD

1 back 1/4″ x 28 1/2″ x 65″

4 drawer bottoms 1/4 ″ x 12 7/8″ x 19 15/16″

UPPER SECTION
CHERRY

(A) 2 ends 7/8″ x 12″ x 48 5/8″

(B) 1 top 7/8″ x 16 1/4″ x 72 1/2″

(C) 2 end stiles 7/8″ x 3″ x 48 5/8″

(D) 1 top rail 7/8″ x 4 5/8″ x 62 3/4″

(E) frieze, 1 pc. 3/8″ x 3 3/8″ x 66 1/2″

(F) friezes, 2 pcs. 3/8″ x 3 3/8″ x 13 1/4″

(G) dentils 1/8″ x 1/4″ x 1 1/8″

(H) 1 stile between doors 7/8″ x 1 1/2″ x 37 1/8″

(I) 1 rail above drawers 7/8″ x 1 1/2″ x 62 3/4″

(J) 1 rail below drawers 7/8″ x 1 1/2″ x 62 3/4″

(K) 8 stiles between drawers 7/8″ x 1″ x 3 1/2″

(L) 9 drawer fronts 5/8″ x 2 1/4″ x 6 1/4″

(M) 2 candlestick holders 7/16″ x 4 7/8″ x 12″

(N) 2 fronts for candlestick holders 7/8″ x 1″ x 5 3/8″

(O) 1 bottom board in back 7/8″ x 8 3/8″ x 65″

(P) 4 door stiles 7/8″ x 1 5/8″ x 35″

(Q) 2 top rails in doors 7/8″ x 4 1/4″ x 27 7/8″

(R) 2 bottom rails in doors 7/8″ x 2 9/16″ x 27 7/8″

(S) 4 muntin rails in doors 7/8″ x 7/8″ x 27 7/8″

(T) 4 muntin stiles in doors 7/8″ x 7/8″ x 7 13/16″

(U) 8 muntin stiles in doors 7/8″ x 7/8″ x 10 1/4″

(V) cornice molding 2 1/4″ x 2 1/4″ x 100 1/2″

(W) 2 quarter columns (from turning shown in fig. 5) 4 pcs. 1″ x 1″ x 35″

(X) molding around bottom 1″ x 1″ x 105″ (approx. length needed)

POPLAR

(Y) 2 tracks for candlestick holders 1″ x 7″ x 11 1/8″

(Z) 1 top rail at back 7/8″ x 4 1/8″ x 65″

1 ceiling and two shelves, 3 pcs. 7/8″ x 11 3/4″

1 shelf above drawers 3/4″ x 11 3/4″ x 64 3/4″

1 shelf below drawers 3/4″ x 11 1/8″ x 64 3/4″

8 drawer guides 3/4″ x 1″ x 11 1/8″

2 drawer guides 3/4″ x 2 1/8″ x 11 1/8″

18 drawer sides 3/8″ x 1 15/16″ x 12″

9 drawer backs 3/8″ x 1 15/16″ x 5 5/8″

BIRCH PLYWOOD

1 back 1/4″ x 48″ x 65″

9 drawer bottoms 1/8″ x 5 1/8″ x 11 1/2″

CHERRY CORNER CUPBOARD

by Franklin H. Gottshall

Corner cupboards are not only of great utilitarian value but are almost invariably beautiful pieces of furniture. One eye-catching feature that makes them attractive is the colorful china so often featured on their shelves. Aside from the decorative quality of the contents usually displayed in full view behind the glass doors of their upper section, the variety of the many attractively designed pieces enhances their distinctive qualities. Furthermore, because they are made to be placed in room corners where few other items of furniture would fit, or play so important a role, their usefulness is enhanced. To sum it all up, corner cupboards are beautiful and useful pieces of furniture and usually do not overcrowd areas of a room they occupy.

Most corner cupboards are built in two sections. This makes it easier to move them should this become necessary. The upper section rests upon the lower section but is not fastened to it. A molding around the top and ends of the lower section keeps the upper section in its proper place. See molding (N) at the top of the lower section in *Figures 2* and *3*.

When building two-section corner cupboards, I prefer making the glass door, or doors, of the upper section first, because it is the more difficult part to make. Once the door has been made it is easier to build the cupboard to conform to the size and shape of the door than it would be to make the door conform to the size of a previously assembled cupboard.

To make the door, cut and plane stock for door stiles (H), top rail (I), bottom rail (J), horizontal and vertical door moldings (K), (L), and (M). Cut mortises in door stiles (H). Then cut tenons on door rails (I), (J), and (K) to fit the mortises in the door stiles. This is done before cutting the molding on the shaper, and before bandsawing the lower edge of rail (I) to shape. The shape of the molding is shown in *Figure 4*.

Figure 1

Once the molding has been cut on stiles and rails, notch the rails where vertical and horizontal moldings are joined. Mortise and tenon joints are used to join rails (I), (J), and (K) to stiles (H). The short vertical muntin moldings (L), and (M) are glued to the notches cut into the horizontal rails. Once the panes of glass are in place, these joints will be strong enough to hold them in place. It should be noted that the surface of rail (I) must be lowered ¼ " in back to hold the tops of the three upper panes of glass. *(See Figure 4)*

When the door has been made, get out stock for posts (A) and (B), and for stiles (C). Grooves 3/8" deep and 3/4" wide are cut across posts (A) where ceiling (P), shelves (O), and floor (N) are glued to posts (A). Post (B) at the back is nailed to the top (F) and to ceiling (P), shelves (O), and floor (N). Top (F) is rabbeted on the underside to fit over post (B) and the two plywood backs, as shown in Figure 3, and its front and ends are molded on a shaper where these edges extend over crown molding (G).

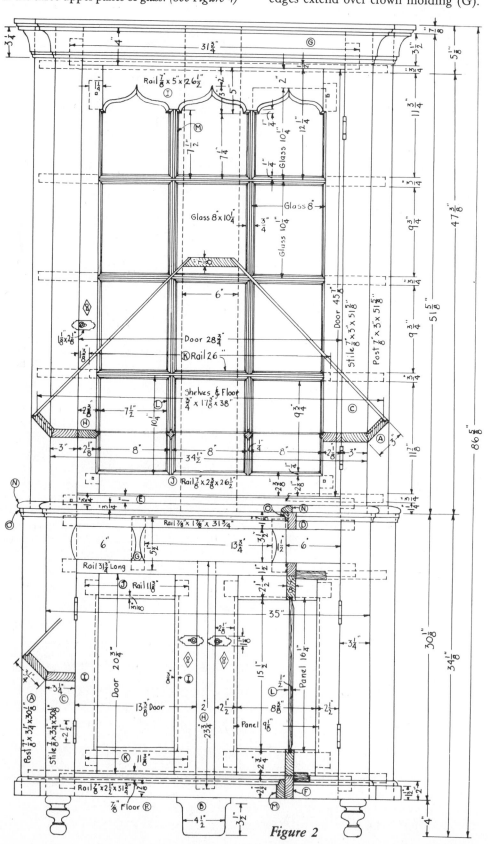

Figure 2

DRAWINGS BY FRANKLIN H. GOTTSHALL

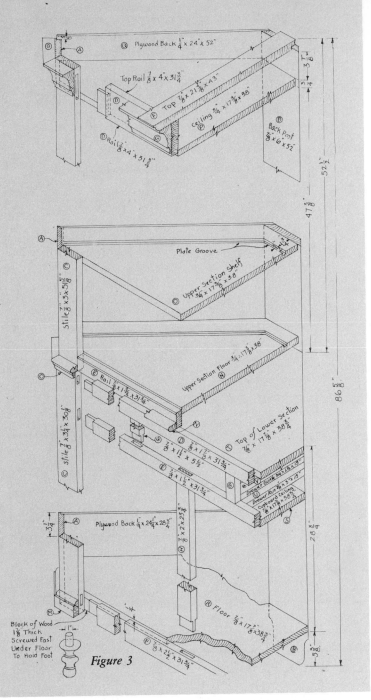

Figure 3

Block of Wood 1⅛" Thick Screwed Fast Under Floor To Hold Foot

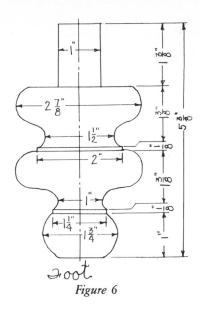

Foot

Figure 6

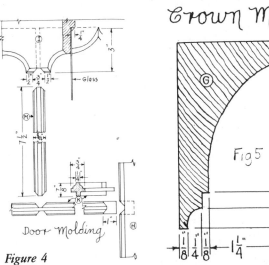

Crown Molding

Door Molding

Figure 4

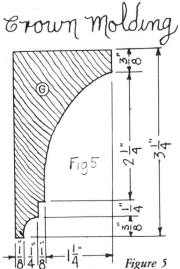

Fig 5

Figure 5

Cut and plane rails (D) and (E), and make the mortises and tenons to join these to stiles (C).

When hinges, locks and latches* have been fitted to doors and stiles, you are ready to make the lower section.

Start the lower section by cutting and shaping posts (A) and (B), and stiles (C). Cut grooves 3/8″ deep across the inside of posts (A) where ends of floor (R), cupboard ceiling (S), and top (T) are joined to the end posts. Make rails (D), (E), and (F). Make stiles (G) to go between the three drawers and also stile (H) which goes between the doors. Make mortise and tenon joints to fasten the rails and stiles together thus forming a frame for the front of the lower section.

Make floor (R) and cupboard ceiling (S). Then make drawer runs (U) and drawer guides (V) and screw these to the top of ceiling (S). Short runs and guides should also be made and fastened to the top of the ceiling to hold and guide the other sides of the short drawers. These are not shown on the drawings. Floor and ceiling may then be glued to posts (A). Glue the assembled front frame to posts (A). Make the top of the lower section (T) which will become the platform upon which the upper section will rest. Place the upper section on this platform and draw lines around it on top of (T) to show where molding (N) should be glued and nailed to keep the upper section where it belongs when placed there.

"I prefer making the glass door first as it's the most difficult..."

Make the doors. Make rails and stiles, and groove the edges to hold the panels. Make mortise and tenon joints, and after fitting the panels, glue rails to stiles to make the doors. Do not glue the panels to the door frames but fit panels so they can swell and shrink about 1/8″ across their width with change of seasons. Fasten hinges, door latches, and locks as shown in Fig. 2.

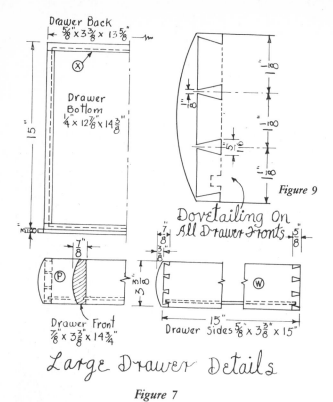

Drawer Back
5/8" x 3 3/8 x 13 5/8"

(X)

Drawer
Bottom
1/4 x 12 7/8 x 14 3/8

15"

Figure 9

Dovetailing On All Drawer Fronts

(P)

Drawer Front
7/8" x 3 3/8 x 14 3/4"

(W)

Drawer Sides 5/8" x 3 3/8 x 15"
15"

Large Drawer Details

Figure 7

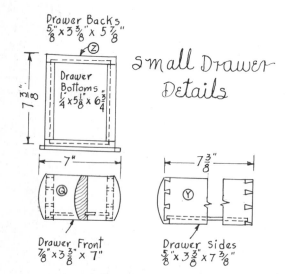

Drawer Backs
5/8" x 3 3/8" x 5 7/8"

(Z)

Drawer
Bottoms
1/4 x 5 1/8 x 6 3/4"

7 3/8"

Small Drawer Details

7"

(Q)

Drawer Front
7/8" x 3 3/8 x 7"

(Y)

Drawer Sides
5/8" x 3 3/8 x 7 3/8"

7 3/8"

Figure 8

Turn the two front feet as shown in Figure 6. Blocks of wood 1 7/8" thick are glued and screwed fast under the floor to fasten the feet.

Make the drawers. Figure 7 shows details for making the large drawer, and Figure 8 for making the small drawers. An enlarged detail showing dovetailing for all three drawers is shown in Figure 9. Be sure these are all properly fitted to slide in and out easily before gluing the dovetail joints, and before the plywood backs of the lower section are nailed fast. Use the finish of your choice depending on the type of wood used.

Door latches may be bought from Ball & Ball, Exton, Pa. Cat #J-25.

BILL OF MATERIAL

UPPER SECTION
Cherry (or mahogany, or walnut)

- (A) 2 posts 7/8" x 3" x 51 5/8"
- (B) 1 back post 7/8" x 6" x 52"
- (C) 2 stiles 7/8" x 3" x 51 5/8"
- (D) 1 top rail above door 7/8" x 4" x 31¾"
- (E) 1 bottom rail below door 7/8" x 1¾" x 31¾"
- (F) 1 top 7/8" x 21 3/8" x 43"
- (G) crown molding 1¾" x 3¼" x 48" (approx)
- (H) 2 door stiles 7/8" x 2 3/8" x 45 7/8"
- (I) 1 top door rail 7/8" x 5" x 26½"
- (J) 1 bottom door rail 7/8" x 2 3/8" x 26½"
- (K) 3 horizontal door muntins ¾" x 7/8" x 26"
- (L) 6 vertical door muntins ¾" x 7/8" x 10¼"
- (M) 2 vertical door muntins ¾" x 7/8" x 7½"

Pine or poplar

- (N) 1 upper section floor ¾" x 17 3/8" x 38"
- (O) 3 upper section shelves ¾" x 17 3/8" x 38"
- (P) 1 upper section ceiling ¾" x 17 3/8" x 38"

Birch Plywood

- (Q) 2 plywood backs ¼" x 24" x 52"

LOWER SECTION
Cherry (or mahogany, or walnut)

- (A) 2 posts 7/8" x 3¼" x 30 1/8"
- (B) 1 back post 7/8" x 6" x 34 1/8"
- (C) 2 stiles 7/8" x 3¼" x 30 1/8"
- (D) 1 rail above drawers 7/8" x 1 7/8" x 31¾"
- (E) 1 rail below drawers 7/8" x 1½" x 31¾"
- (F) 1 rail below doors 7/8" x 2½" x 31¾"
- (G) 2 short stiles between drawers 7/8" x 1½" x 5½"
- (H) 1 stile between doors 7/8" x 2" x 23¾"
- (I) 4 door stiles 7/8" x 2½" x 20¾"
- (J) 2 top rails on doors 7/8" x 2½" x 11 3/8"
- (K) 2 bottom rails on doors 7/8" x 2¾" x 11 3/8"
- (L) 2 panels on doors ½" x 9 1/8" x 16¼"
- (M) molding on bottom rail 7/8" x 2" x 43" (approx)
- (N) molding around top of lower section ¾" x 1¼" x 43" (approx)
- (O) molding under (N) ½" x ¾" x 43" (approx)
- (P) 1 large drawer front 7/8" x 3 3/8" x 14¾"
- (Q) 2 small drawer fronts 7/8" x 3 3/8" x 7"
  2 feet 2 7/8" diam x 5 3/8"

Pine or Poplar

- (R) 1 floor 7/8" x 17 7/8" x 38¾"
- (S) 1 cupboard ceiling 7/8" x 17 7/8" x 38¾"
- (T) 1 top of lower section 7/8" x 17 7/8" x 38¾"
- (U) 2 drawer runs 7/8" x 3" x 15"
- (V) 2 drawer guides ¾" x 1½" x 15"
- (W) 2 drawer sides 5/8" x 3 3/8" x 15"
- (X) 1 drawer back 5/8" x 3 3/8" x 13 5/8"
- (Y) 4 drawer sides 5/8" x 3 3/8" x 7 3/8"
- (Z) 2 drawer backs 5/8" x 3 3/8" x 5 7/8"

Birch Plywood

2 backs for lower section ¼" x 24¼" x 28¾"
1 drawer bottom ¼" x 12 7/8" x 14 3/8"
2 drawer bottoms ¼" x 5 1/8" x 6¾"

ABOUT THE AUTHOR:

Franklin H. Gottshall is a contributing editor to The American Woodworker.

TOY HUTCH

by John A. Nelson

This toy hutch was found on the top of a heap of trash in a dump in northern Vermont. Except for broken glass and two cracked door panels, it was complete and in excellent condition. It seemed a shame to let it rot there so I brought it home for my six-year-old daughter. The moment I saw it, I knew she would like it. I was right, and now, even after eight years, she still makes good use of it. Over the past eight years the toys neatly placed on the shelves have changed and become more and more ''grownup''. Today the hutch is still a very important part of my daughter's life, and, in a way, it has matured with her, at least in content. In years to come, I'll bet my daughter will give this toy hutch to her daughter.

As the small 1″ x 2¼″ celluloid name tab, neatly attached to the back of the top trim with four brass nails, indicates, the hutch was commercially manufactured. The tab reads:

> Manufactured for
> F.A.O. Schwarz
> TOYS
> Fifth Avenue and Thirty First Street,
> New York

Because of the pre-plastic celluloid tab, I would estimate the hutch to have been made between 1920 and 1930. Perhaps a reader could shed some light on this.

The hutch is built of two complete assemblies held together by two flat head wood screws. Construction of the top assembly and the bottom assembly is very simple with only butt joints used throughout. Only the two back boards were rabbeted into the side panels. All joints were glued and nailed together with small finish nails.

As with any project, carefully cut all boards to size per the bill of materials list. Some boards will have to be glued up to size and others will have to be planed to correct thickness. All size dimensions have been carefully checked and re-checked, but it is a good idea to dry-fit all parts to re-check correctness of fit before final assembly.

After putting the two assemblies together, sand all over and seal before applying the finish coat of paint. The hutch can be painted any color, but the original was painted a satin white. Because

PHOTO BY DEBORAH PORTER

this will be used by a child, it would be a good idea to paint it with a non-toxic paint. For safety sake, in place of the glass, it is recommended that two pieces of plexi-glass be used. This will not be noticed after assembly.

The drawer unit is constructed with a simple rabbet joint in the front board and a simple 1/8″ dado along the sides for the bottom board. The front board was the only part of the drawer assembly that was painted. Very inexpensive drawer pulls were used, in fact, very inexpensive hardware was used throughout the hutch.

Doors stops were simply large headed brass tacks left high enough to cause friction to hold the doors closed. Small bullet-type catches would work a little better today.

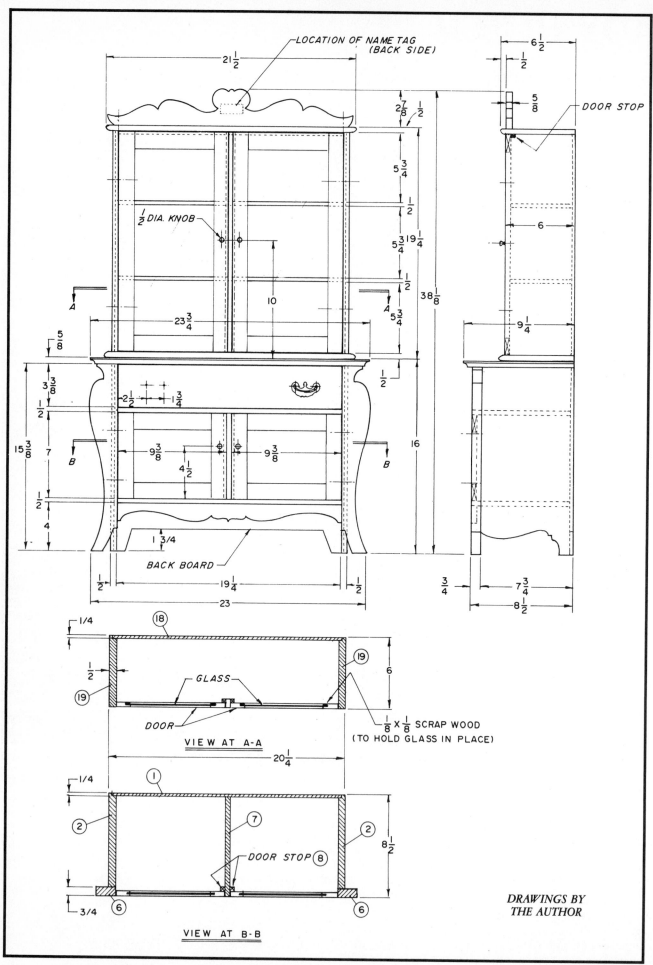

LOCATION OF NAME TAG
(BACK SIDE)

$21\frac{1}{2}$

$6\frac{1}{2}$

$\frac{1}{2}$

$\frac{5}{8}$

DOOR STOP

$2\frac{7}{8}$ $\frac{1}{2}$

$5\frac{3}{4}$

$\frac{1}{2}$

$\frac{1}{2}$ DIA. KNOB

$5\frac{3}{4}$ $19\frac{1}{4}$

6

$\frac{1}{2}$

A

A

10

$38\frac{1}{8}$

$5\frac{3}{4}$

$23\frac{3}{4}$

$9\frac{1}{4}$

$\frac{5}{8}$

$\frac{1}{2}$

$3\frac{3}{8}$

$\frac{1}{2}$

$2\frac{1}{2}$ $1\frac{3}{4}$

$15\frac{3}{8}$

7

B

B

$9\frac{3}{8}$

$9\frac{3}{8}$

16

$4\frac{1}{2}$

$\frac{1}{2}$

4

$1\frac{3}{4}$

BACK BOARD

$\frac{1}{2}$

$19\frac{1}{4}$

$\frac{1}{2}$

$\frac{3}{4}$

$7\frac{3}{4}$

23

$8\frac{1}{2}$

1/4

⑱

⑲

$\frac{1}{2}$

6

GLASS

⑲

DOOR

$\frac{1}{8} \times \frac{1}{8}$ SCRAP WOOD
(TO HOLD GLASS IN PLACE)

VIEW AT A-A

$20\frac{1}{4}$

1/4

①

②

⑦

②

$8\frac{1}{2}$

DOOR STOP ⑧

3/4

⑥

⑥

*DRAWINGS BY
THE AUTHOR*

VIEW AT B-B

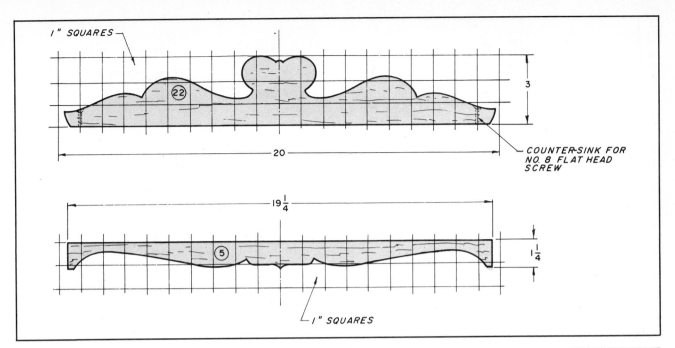

1" SQUARES

22

3

20

COUNTER-SINK FOR
NO. 8 FLAT HEAD
SCREW

$19\frac{1}{4}$

5

$1\frac{1}{4}$

1" SQUARES

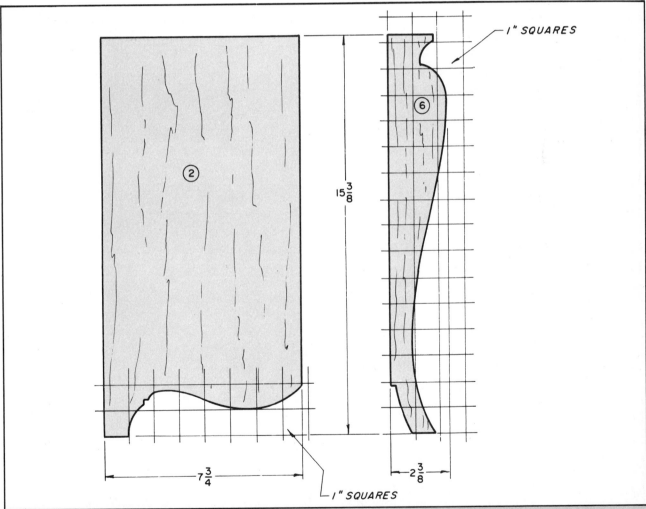

1" SQUARES

6

2

$15\frac{3}{8}$

$7\frac{3}{4}$

$2\frac{3}{8}$

1" SQUARES

When the two assemblies are finished and painted, line up the two back surfaces and center the top assembly upon the bottom assembly and screw the parts together with two, 1" long flat head screws.

You now have a toy that may become more than just a toy. You may have created an heirloom to be passed down for many years to come.

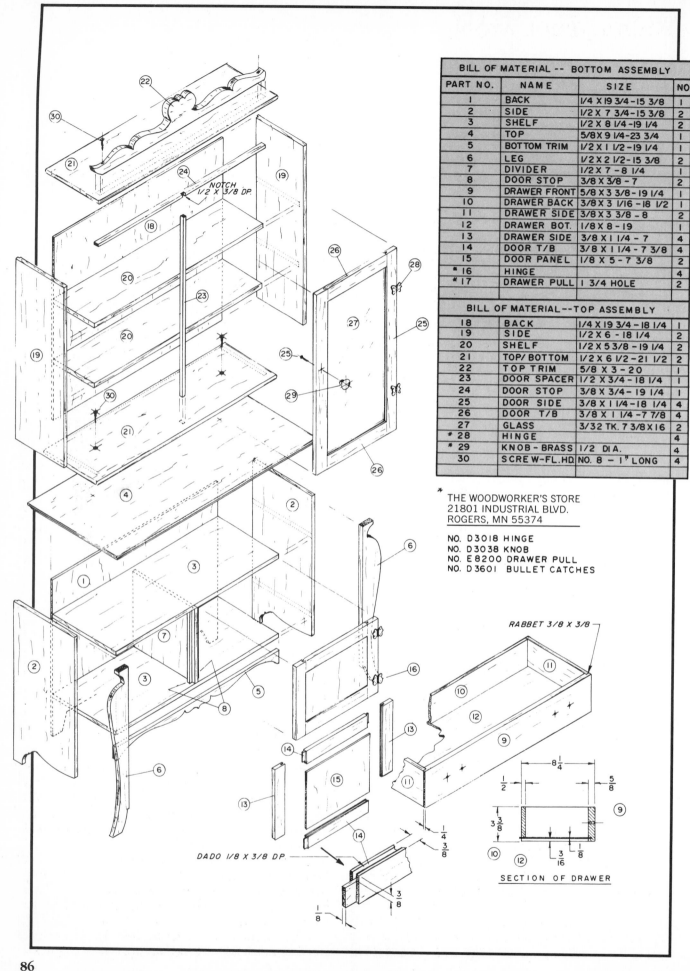

BILL OF MATERIAL -- BOTTOM ASSEMBLY			
PART NO.	NAME	SIZE	NO
1	BACK	1/4 X 19 3/4 -15 3/8	1
2	SIDE	1/2 X 7 3/4 -15 3/8	2
3	SHELF	1/2 X 8 1/4 -19 1/4	2
4	TOP	5/8 X 9 1/4 -23 3/4	1
5	BOTTOM TRIM	1/2 X 1 1/2 -19 1/4	1
6	LEG	1/2 X 2 1/2 -15 3/8	2
7	DIVIDER	1/2 X 7 - 8 1/4	1
8	DOOR STOP	3/8 X 3/8 - 7	2
9	DRAWER FRONT	5/8 X 3 3/8 -19 1/4	1
10	DRAWER BACK	3/8 X 3 1/16 -18 1/2	1
11	DRAWER SIDE	3/8 X 3 3/8 - 8	2
12	DRAWER BOT.	1/8 X 8 -19	1
13	DRAWER SIDE	3/8 X 1 1/4 - 7	4
14	DOOR T/B	3/8 X 1 1/4 - 7 3/8	4
15	DOOR PANEL	1/8 X 5 - 7 3/8	2
* 16	HINGE		4
* 17	DRAWER PULL	1 3/4 HOLE	2

BILL OF MATERIAL -- TOP ASSEMBLY			
18	BACK	1/4 X 19 3/4 -18 1/4	1
19	SIDE	1/2 X 6 -18 1/4	2
20	SHELF	1/2 X 5 3/8 -19 1/4	2
21	TOP/ BOTTOM	1/2 X 6 1/2 -21 1/2	2
22	TOP TRIM	5/8 X 3 -20	1
23	DOOR SPACER	1/2 X 3/4 -18 1/4	1
24	DOOR STOP	3/8 X 3/4 -19 1/4	1
25	DOOR SIDE	3/8 X 1 1/4 -18 1/4	4
26	DOOR T/B	3/8 X 1 1/4 -7 7/8	4
27	GLASS	3/32 TK. 7 3/8 X 16	2
* 28	HINGE		4
* 29	KNOB - BRASS	1/2 DIA.	4
30	SCREW-FL.HD	NO. 8 - 1" LONG	4

* THE WOODWORKER'S STORE
21801 INDUSTRIAL BLVD.
ROGERS, MN 55374

NO. D3018 HINGE
NO. D3038 KNOB
NO. E8200 DRAWER PULL
NO. D3601 BULLET CATCHES

NOTCH 1/2 X 3/8 DP.

RABBET 3/8 X 3/8

DADO 1/8 X 3/8 DP.

8 1/4

1/2

5/8

3 3/8

3/16

1/8

1/4

3/8

3/8

1/8

SECTION OF DRAWER

Walnut Foot Stool

by Dennis R. Watson

Relaxing in your favorite chair with your feet on this contemporary walnut stool, a bowl of popcorn in your lap, and you're ready for this week's ball game. Construction needs include conventional blind mortise and tenon joints, and spline-strengthened miter joints. The really fun part of the project starts when you get out the gouges and surform to shape and blend the legs and rails. Upholstering the seat is not difficult; it's a simple cover sewn together at the corners, pulled over a foam covered plywood board, and stapled in place.

The legs and top rail require a 2 1/2 inch by 1 3/4 inch piece of walnut which is expensive and difficult to find, so I used 1 1/4 inch thick walnut and glued a 3/4

inch thick strip three inches long to the top of the legs *(Figure 1)* and each end of the top rails, and a 1/2 X 3 inch back to the legs where the seat rail joins. The additional strips of wood provide enough thickness to cut the radius or curved corners. Miter the ends of the legs and top rail, then cut the mortises for the lower rail and seat rail. I cut the mortises on the radial arm saw using a 1/4 inch bottoming end mill and a shopmade jig. The mortises could also be cut with a router or by hand with a chisel. If you prefer, dowels could be substituted for the mortise and tenon joint.

Rip the stock for the stretcher from 1/2 inch walnut and the seat rail from 1/2 inch walnut. Cut to length and

FOOT STOOL

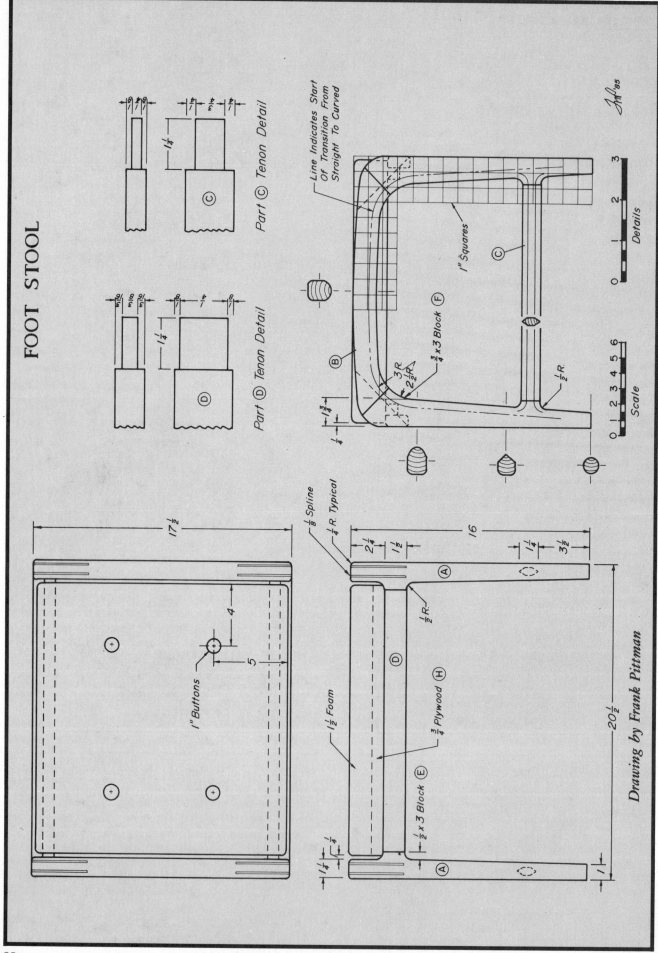

Drawing by Frank Pittman

don't forget to allow for the tenons. Cut the tenons on the table saw or radial arm saw a little fat, then trim with a sharp chisel to fit snuggly in the mortises.

At this time you can bandsaw the interior radius of the legs and upper rail. Don't bandsaw the exterior radius until after glue up; the square corners aid in clamping. If you don't have a bandsaw and are using a saber saw, it's just as easy to wait and make the interior cuts after glue up *(Figure 2)*. Dry fit the ends together and make sure the joints pull up tight, then add glue and clamp overnight.

Fig. 2 After the end frame has dried, cut the taper and radius corners using a saber saw. A band saw can be used for all exterior cuts.

Fig. 1 Small blocks of walnut are glued to the 1 1/4 inch thick leg to provide enough wood from which to cut the radius corners.

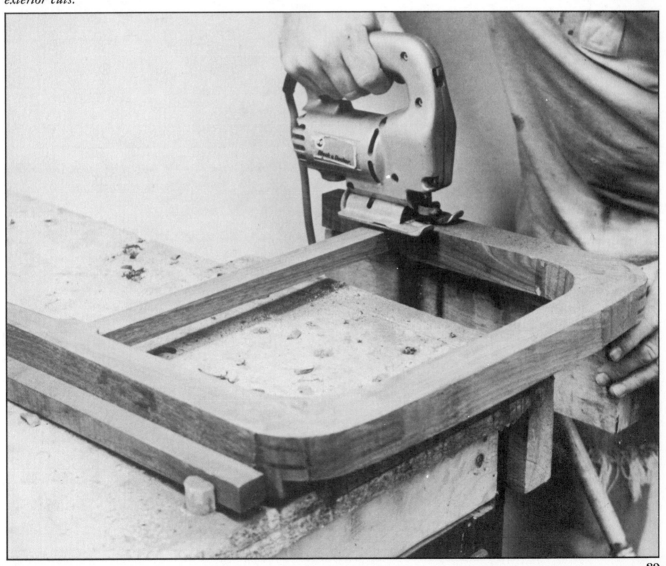

The real strength of the miter joint lies in the two 1/8 inch triangular splines. I cut the 1/8 inch slots for the splines using a 10 inch carbide tip combination blade on the table saw. A shopmade tenoning jig (see *The American Woodworker,* Vol. I, No. II) is used to hold the end frame vertical. The frame is clamped to the jig, and the jig and frame slide along the rip fence past the saw blade *(Figure 3)*. Cut two slots in each corner. The splines should fit snugly in the groove. If they're too tight, the wood will swell when glue is applied, and you'll not be able to drive in the splines. The splines could be made from contrasting wood, such as oak or cherry, for an interesting visual effect. Glue the splines in place. Use a "C" clamp across the face with small blocks to prevent the clamp from marring the surface and to distribute the pressure.

Now comes the fun part, the shaping. I used carving gouges and a round surform to rough out the work. The rough surfaces were smoothed using a small flap type sander and 1/2 inch diameter drum sander, both mounted in a 1/4 inch drill *(Figure 4)*. Final sanding was done by hand using 220 grit sandpaper.

With the ends finished, the seat rail is next. It's made from 3/4 inch thick stock. Cut the tenon on each end and dry fit the seat rail to both end frames; check to make sure the joints pull up tight. Apply glue and clamp. Check to be sure the assembly is square. Use a surform and a 1/2 inch sanding drum to smooth the corner between the end frame and seat rail *(Figure 6)*.

Fig. 4 A rotary rasp chucked in a drill is a quick way to smooth the radius corner between the leg and lower rail.

Fig. 3 The miter joints are strengthened with two 1/8 inch thick splines. Cut the grooves using a 10 inch combination blade and shopmade tenoning jig.

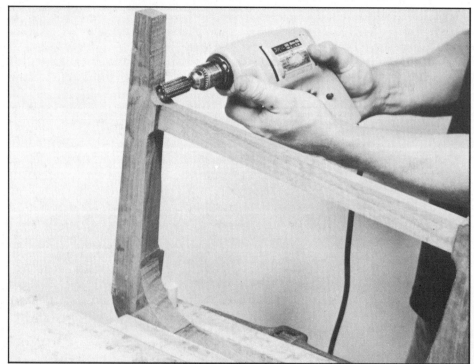

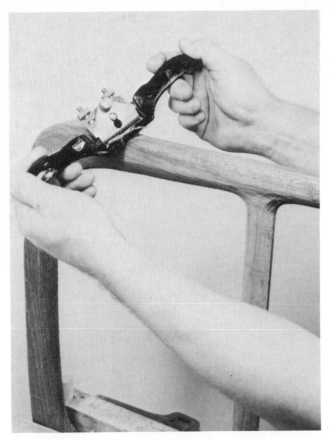

Fig. 5   Shape the outside of the leg with a spokeshave. The top of the leg is rectangular in cross section and changes to a circle at the bottom.

Fig. 6   A round surform is used to smooth the tool marks left by the carving gouge.

Cut a piece of 3/4 inch plywood to size and drill several holes in it to allow air to escape from the cushion. Glue medium density foam to the plywood using rubber cement. Now cut the upholstery to size and sew the box corners. Next, stretch the fabric over the foam and plywood, and staple in place. Have one inch buttons covered at a local upholstery shop with the same upholstery fabric used to cover the stool. Drill a 1/8 inch hole in the plywood bottom at the location of the button. Attach heavy weight string to the button, and using a long upholstery needle, probe for the hole. Pull the string through and tie off.

For a professional looking job, use tack strip to apply upholstery to the underside of the bottom. It covers the exposed wood and stapled edges.

Attach a 3/4 x 3/4 inch ledger strip to the seat rails using No. 6 x 1 1/4 inch flat head screws. Then screw the seat to the ledger with No. 6 x 1 1/4 inch flat head screws.

The stool is finished using two coats of Watco Danish Oil with the second coat wet sanded using number 600 wet/dry sandpaper. The oil is followed with a coat of paste wax to finish the project.

CUTTING LIST

PIECE	QUANTITY	SIZE			DESCRIPTION
A	4	1 3/4" x	1 1/4" x	16"	Walnut leg
B	2	1 3/4" x	1 1/4" x	17 1/2"	Walnut top rail
C	2	1/2" x	1 1/4" x	16 1/2"	Walnut stretcher
D	2	3/4" x	1 1/2" x	19 1/2"	Walnut seat rail
E	4	1/2" x	3/4" x	3"	Walnut block
F	8	3/4" x	1 1/4" x	3"	Walnut block
G	2	3/4" x	3/4" x	18"	Walnut ledger
H	1	3/4" x	17 1/2" x	17"	Fir plywood seat

ABOUT THE AUTHOR:

Dennis Watson is an amateur woodworker and contributing editor to **The American Woodworker.** *He makes his living as an aerospace engineer.*

Photos by the Author

A Modified LC Table

by Pat Warner

This spartan white oak table design represents simple solutions to some complicated problems. The spindly members best conceived in bent steel tubing designs of Mies Van Der Rohe, Breuer, and Le Corbusier do not readily lend themselves to conventional woodworking techniques. However, there are certain geometric advantages in continuous steel tube configurations that are shared equally well in wood that help compensate.

For example, the tops are structural elements. The frames, though well joined and reinforced, need the tops to complete their cycle of strength. The solid wood slab top is cut to 18″ in width. Throughout the seasons it can be expected to expand and contract ³⁄₁₆″. The tandem leg sets can easily flex to accommodate the change yet handily resist the deflection caused by an accidental kick.

The long 1″ diameter rails are easily bent if loose in the hand. However, as part of the assembly, the rails and the top compliment each other to provide an inflexible element.

Its weak point, the leg to long rail junction, has been compensated for in two ways. The first is the joint itself. The rail has shouldered tenons so the full diameter of the rail is under load when stressed—not just the smaller diameter tenoned section. Secondly, the legs are in tandem by virtue of the floor rail so forces exerted on one leg are shared by both.

To be sure, this table is not designed for weight lifting or bench pressing, but it is substantial and does offer a simple solution to facilitate a decorating problem.

To start out, make the end assemblies since they are the most difficult. They are formed with a glue joint and dowels, but dovetailing or double splining and doweling will work just as well. The legs should measure 18″ - 22″ for easier router maneuvering while the floor rails' length must be

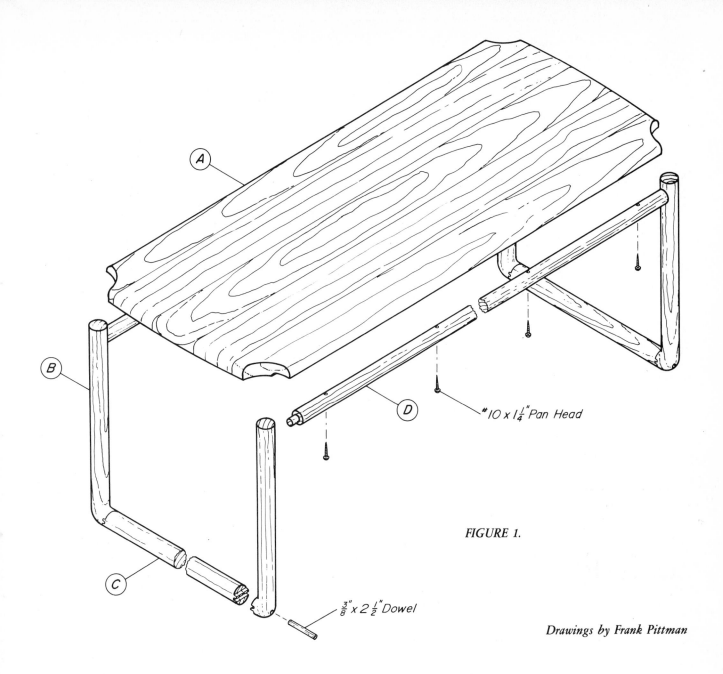

A

B

C

D

#10 x 1¼" Pan Head

FIGURE 1.

⅜" x 2½" Dowel

Drawings by Frank Pittman

dimensioned for the U-assembly to net 17⅝" as its final outside dimension. (See Fig. 1)

The end (U) assemblies are routed round from square sectioned material after glue up. The reason for this lies in the sculpted corners. The radius in the inside corners is there essentially for design purposes to copy the look you'd expect in bent steel tubing. Though the process is complex and messy, the result is clean and inspiring.

To make the leg rail elements, glue joint the ends of the floor rail to the legs and through dowel the corners with ⅜" × 2½" long dowels. Flush template rout a radius of ¹³⁄₁₆ to the outside corners. (See Fig. 2) These 3 members measure 1⁹⁄₁₆" × 1¼" in section, and if a ⁵⁄₁₆" rabbet is applied to the inside of the glued assembly, it will swing (create) an inside corner radius of ½" in section after the uncut portion of the rabbet is wasted away. In addition, the elements are rendered 1¼" square (1⁹⁄₁₆" − ⁵⁄₁₆" = 1¼") so if a ⅝" radius round over bit is put to each of the four corners, the ''bent-tube look'' is achieved. (See Fig. 3) The legs are left

long (2" - 4") so the assembly can be screwed down to a substrate and routed (portably) from end to end without hitting clamps. After routing and sanding, trim the legs to net 16⅛" and prepare to bore the mortices and counterbores for the long rails.

> *Though the process is complex*
> *and messy, the result*
> *is clean and inspiring.*

The holes are best drilled with a counterbore bradpoint drill combination to facilitate concentricity. The holes (mortices) are centered and 1⅛" from the leg end. To locate this (using a drill press) without going through the headaches of scribing the rounds, mark a flat square ended stick 1⅛" × ⅝" from any corner and drill a hole in the stick there, lock the quill and locate stops (fences) on the end and side of this scrap stick. Now when you butt the leg ends into the pocket formed by the stops, the holes will automatically be located. A 1″ counterbore should be drilled to ⁵⁄₁₆″ and a ½″ diameter hole to 1¹⁄₁₆″ (see Fig. 4). This completes the machine work for the end assemblies.

Next make the long rails (spindles, in this case). Cut 1″ square material 44″ - 48″ long and round all four corners with a ½″ radius round over bit. Sand the rounds with a covered sanding block, then cut to net 41¹⁄₁₆″. With the spindle on end, form ¾″ long ¼″ shouldered ½″ diameter tenons with a ¼″ router rabbet bit (see Fig. 5). Next drill and counterbore the spindle to receive four #10 × 1¼″ panhead sheet metal screws

FIGURE 2

A ⁵⁄₁₆″ rabbeting bit with an outside diameter of 1″ is used to form a ½″ corner radius. The uncut portion of the rabbet should be trimmed flush with a flush trimmer bit.

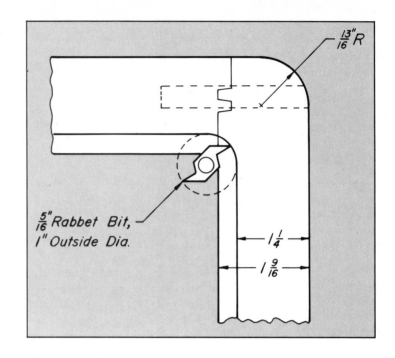

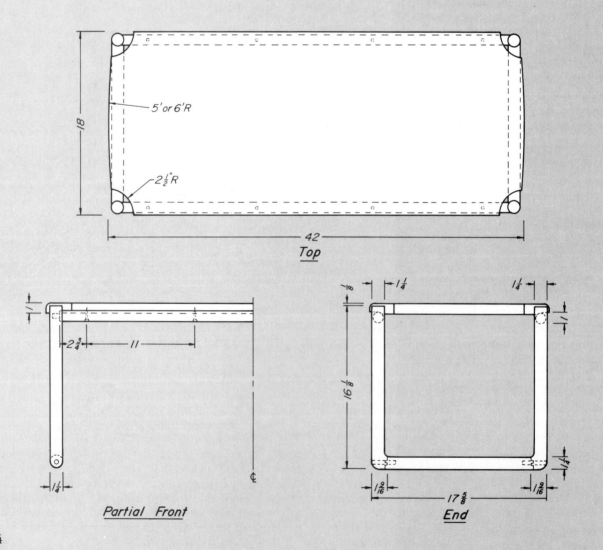

Top

Partial Front

End

94

It might be wise to put a drill rod in one of the holes during assembly

which hold the top in place. (See fig. 6) This is a little tricky because the spindle tends to roll and therefore the axis of each succeeding hole could be different. To keep the holes aligned, use two sets of counterbores and drills as follows. Locate the hole distances 2¾" from the tenon shoulder on either end and 11" in from both of these holes. Find the center of the round as before (with the 1¼" material), but this time use only one stop (fence) ½" from the drill point center line. Place the spindle on a ½" (or less) thick, narrow (less than 6") piece of scrap ply as long (or longer) than the spindle. Drill the first hole and lock the quill at full depth. Remove the drill and counterbore from the chuck leaving it and the spindle impaled on the ply—this establishes the axis for the rest of the holes. Drill the next hole with the other drill / counterbore set and again leave the drill stuck through the spindle into the ply. Remove drill number one and repeat until all eight holes are drilled. The spindles now can be glued to the U-assemblies. It might be wise to put a drill rod in one of the holes during assembly to help sight in the vertical axis in case you have drilled aligned holes in vain.

To highlight more of the bent tube look, round the edges and ends on both sides

The top is the next element of the structure. Glue up material to achieve a 1" thick slab 18" × 42". Jig saw and template route a gentle (5' -6') radius on the ends of the slab. (See Fig. 1) To highlight more of the bent tube look, round the edges and ends on both sides with a ½" round over bit. I didn't like the overall thickness of the top and rail on the side elevation, so I wasted ⅜" of it to about 1⁵⁄₁₆" inboard. The top is sized to overhang ⁵⁄₁₆" on both sides and ⁹⁄₃₂" past the legs on the ends. This waste is only along the sides and allows the top to rest ⅜" lower on the rails, thus diminishing that overall thickness. Do this with a router and a 1" diameter core box bit and clamp down board (see Fig. 7). Finally, notch (template rout) the corners with 2½" radii to clear the leg ends, locate and transfer punch the rail holes to the underside of the top and drill ¹¹⁄₆₄" × ½" deep holes to receive the #10 screws.

The whole affair was Watco wet sanded, wiped clean and then waxed.

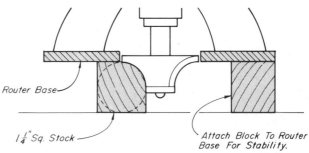

FIGURE 3.

A ⅝" rounding over bit used to form the radius on 1¼" square stock. Note that the block is attached to the router base for stability.

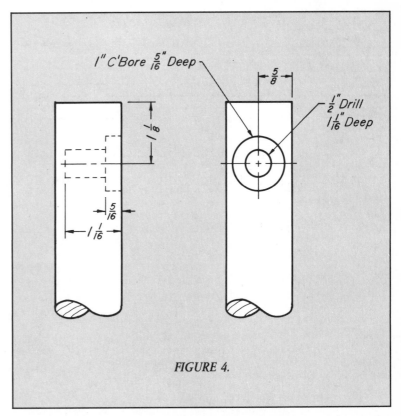

FIGURE 4.

Leg detail showing mortise for rail.

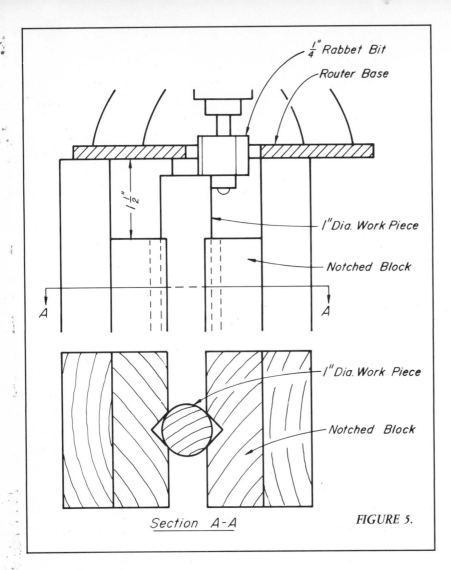

¼" Rabbet Bit

Router Base

½"

1" Dia. Work Piece

Notched Block

1" Dia. Work Piece

Notched Block

Section A-A

FIGURE 5.

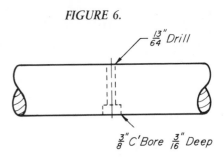

FIGURE 6.

13/64" Drill

3/8" C'Bore 3/16" Deep

Detail of holes through rails for top fastening.

Shop made holder used to form ½" tenons on the end of 1" diameter rails. Secure the holder in a vise and rotate the rabbeting bit around the stock. Lower the cutter until a ¾" tenon is formed.

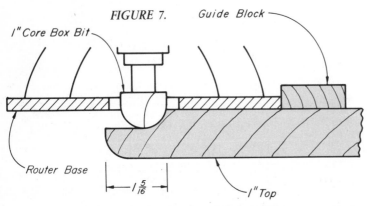

FIGURE 7.

1" Core Box Bit

Guide Block

Router Base

1 5/16"

1" Top

A one inch core box bit is used to undercut the top. The router is guided by a block clamped to the top.

BILL OF MATERIALS

Code	Part	Quan.	T	x	W	x	L	
A	Top	1	1"	x	18"	x	42"	
B	Leg	4	1¼"	x	1⁹⁄₁₆"	x	18" - 22"	RGH (16⅛" Fin.)
C	Floor Rail	2	1¼"	x	1⁹⁄₁₆"	x	14½"	(See note below)*
D	Long Rail	2	1"	x	1"	x	44" - 48"	RGH (41¹⁄₁₆" Fin.)

*Length of floor rail depends upon the type of joint used.

REFERENCES

Le Corbusier (the LC in the title), 1887-1965, is regarded by some as the father of bent steel tubular furniture.

¼" rabbet cutter with ⅜" O.D. bearing (TA 224) — Paso Robles Carbide, 713C Paso Robles St., Paso Robles, CA 93446

Source for drills and counterbores — W.L. Fuller Inc., 7 Cypress St., P.O. Box 8767, Warwick, R.I. 02888

⅜" radius roundover cutter. See #2 or Furnima Industrial Carbide, Inc., Box 308, Biernacki Rd., Barry's Bay, Ontario, Canada K0J 1B0

ABOUT THE AUTHOR: *Pat Warner is a designer and furniture maker in Escondido, CA.*